MARK A. GAEDE *and*
NAOMI GAEDE-PENNER

. . . .

Prescription for Adventure

the ALASKA BUSH PILOT'S SON

The Story of Mark A. Gaede

The Alaska Bush Pilot's Son: The Story of Mark A. Gaede
Published by Prescription for Adventure
Denver, CO

ISBN: 978-0-9637030-3-3
BIOGRAPHY / Aviation & Nautical

Cover photo taken by Naomi Gaede-Penner of Mark Gaede with his Piper PA-18 Super Cub on Iceberg Lake, Kenai Peninsula, Alaska

Alaska map by Barbara Spohn-Lillo

Maps of Bell's fish site at Silver Salmon, and aerials of the Gaede homestead and surrounding areas, by Mark A. Gaede

Propeller sketch by Kenya Jo Gaede

Photos in the Silver Salmon Chapter courtesy of the Wayne and Sandy Bell family

Other photos throughout the book by Elmer E. Gaede and Naomi Gaede-Penner

Cover and Interior design by Victoria Wolf, wolfdesignandmarketing.com

OTHER BOOKS BY
NAOMI GAEDE PENNER

Alaska Bush Pilot Doctor

The Bush Doctor's Wife

From Kansas Wheat Fields to Alaska Tundra:
a Mennonite Family Finds Home

'A' is for Alaska: Teacher to the Territory

'A' is for Anaktuvuk: Teacher to the Nunamiut Eskimos

This book is dedicated to those men and women who grew up on the Kenai Peninsula in the 1960s and 70s. While the stories are specifically mine, some of them could just as well have been theirs. —Mark

Mark, for decades, your stories have captivated my attention. You are my hero. Now these astonishing adventures can be shared with others. —Naomi

CONTENTS

HOW THE BOOK
CAME TO BE

NAOMI:

In 1988, I thought I'd write one book, *Prescription for Adventure: Bush Pilot Doctor*, about my father. I was naïve about the amount of work required to do so, and I vowed never to write another book as long as I lived. Then, I was asked, "What about…?" and I wrote *From Kansas Wheat Fields to Alaska Tundra*.

After a while, I discovered more "prescriptions" for adventure and subsequently put together a grid of stories, main characters, flashbacks, and eras for future books. That was decades ago. Now, with five "Prescription for Adventure" books behind me, this book is in the last column.

Grids, ideas, and passions can be noble or vices or problems. In this case, my passion involved getting my brother to move his eyes from rifle crosshairs and airplane altimeter readings to story writing, stories I believed readers would find incredible, intriguing, and heartwarming.

Over the years, I collected faxes, emails, and conversations from my brother—tidbits of stories. In 2021, I persuaded him to spend two weeks at my home in Denver to sort through slips of paper and organize them into a sequence of events. He started writing. Then he returned home and continued homesteading, dredging gold, writing music, flying, and doing all those activities that feed his soul. In 2022, he flew out again and for two weeks wrote snippets of stories, after which he returned to…yes, *his* passions.

Finally, in January 2024, I captured him and imprisoned him in my basement. He wrote and wrote, and we talked and talked, and we walked and talked, and he wrote, and I edited, and we developed and maintained momentum to push this book to publication.

Working with him on this book and learning what he was like back then has been enlightening, fun, and also sad. I have grieved what I missed by being absent during his grade school and adolescent years. Truly this project has been a gift to me—from him.

MARK:

Naomi and I have different perspectives on my growing-up years on the homestead. Some of that is because she is older than me. In addition, she ended up attending high school in the Lower 48, as well as college. Then she married an "Outsider" and never returned to live in Alaska.

When she began writing about our family history, as documented in her earlier books, she occasionally asked me about Dad's exploits and wanted to know what I remembered. I provided her with details, and since I inherited Dad's bent for storytelling, I added snatches of my stories as well; these she dutifully kept in hard copy.

When we first discussed turning my recollections into another book in her series, I doubted I could come up with enough material. After all, how much could I recall of events buried beneath more than 50 years of life? As it turned out, the quantity of material was not an issue. As I began writing in earnest, one memory triggered another.

Even though I wrote these stories from vivid early experiences, in most instances they were confirmed by Mom and Dad's letters to relatives in the Lower 48, hundreds of Dad's photographs, interviews with individuals who had shared in these stories, pouring over maps, and paging through local news archive. I admit. I have an overactive imagination, so it was reassuring when external sources verified my recollections. Yes, there was an instance where I incorrectly identified an adult in a story, but hey, I was only nine years old at the time, so don't be too harsh.

Most importantly, this book would have never happened if Naomi had not been the driving force behind it. Rumors that she locked me in her Colorado basement and forced me to write are not entirely true—the door to the basement was not locked. Even though I did my writing down there, the struggle up the steps at the end of a writing session was due to the extra pounds I put on from overconsumption of her delectable cooking and baking. Encompassing this endeavor has been her gentle guidance and coaching on how to write, rewrite, and rewrite some more. However, I now cannot read a book or news article without tripping on overused descriptors, misspelled or missing words, and inconsistent verb tenses. Thanks, sis.

INTRODUCTION

DAD STOMPED ON THE SNOW to deepen the track, then took the next step. Neither of us said a word. We moved deliberately. I began thinking that climbing back up and around the snowfield, even with a pack, might have been a better idea. But here we were.

About halfway across the snowfield, and as he took another step, Dad's feet abruptly flew out from under him. I gasped in disbelief as he accelerated down the mountainside on the hard-crusted snow. Snow sprayed everywhere as he dug in his heels. Desperately, he rammed the butt of the rifle into the snow. It did nothing to slow his rapid plunge. About 100 yards downslope, the icy snow terminated into a pile of rocks. Dad slammed into the rocks, bounced in the air, and disappeared over a cliff. I stood utterly still, transfixed by what had just occurred.

Dad was gone! As a 14-year-old, I was alone on a treacherous snowslide. What was I going to do? I visualized Dad's battered body on the glacier thousands of feet below me. I had some time at the controls of the J-3, but could I fly myself home to get help? How was I going to get off this snow? Would I be the next to fall?

ALASKA

*Soldotna, site of the Gaede homestead

Anchorage

Chickaloon Flats

Grey Cliffs

Hope

Cooper Landing

Soldotna

Skilak Lake

Seward

Port Alsworth

Ninilchik

Silver Salmon Creek

Pedro Bay

Anchor Point

Cook Inlet

Homer

Pope Vannoy Landing

Augustine Island

Seldovia

Nanwalek

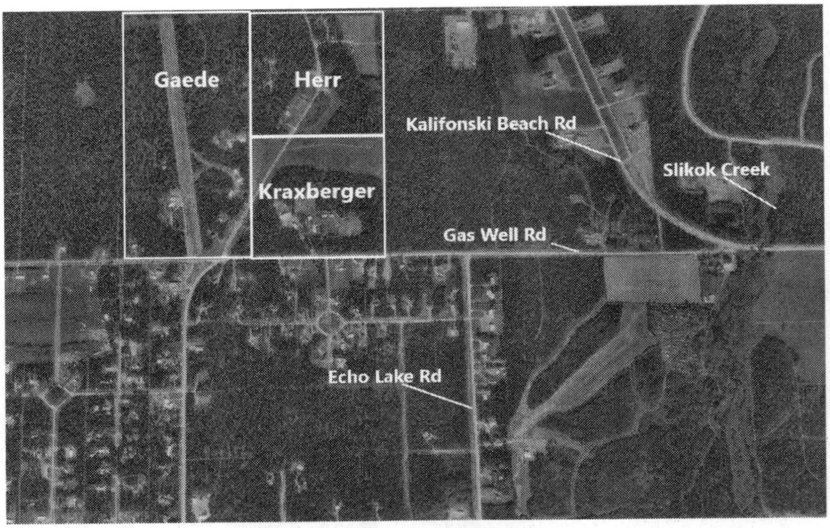
Gaede
Herr
Kraxberger
Kalifonski Beach Rd
Slikok Creek
Gas Well Rd
Echo Lake Rd

Gaede Homestead and Nearby Areas

CHAPTER 1
BEGINNINGS OF A HOMESTEADER

AS WITH MOST YOUNG KIDS, I lived in the moment. A day or two in the future was as far as my time horizon extended. I was just an Alaskan boy on an Alaskan homestead. My dad cut down trees, shoveled snow off our house roof, plugged in the VW bus in the winter so it would start at minus 30 degrees, and flew an airplane—just like many other Alaskans. Mom worked alongside Dad in the woods, kept the fireplace stoked, and learned to cook with canned and boxed products instead of the fresh produce she had enjoyed at her Kansas farm. Both of them were undaunted by hard work, a rugged environment, and brutal winter weather. They honored God and cared about the people around them. As the son of Elmer and Ruby Gaede, this environment is where my story begins.

Our 80-acre homestead sits in the middle of the Kenai (KEEN-eye) Peninsula, 70 miles south of Anchorage, as the eagle flies. By the time I arrived on this piece of land, I had already traveled thousands of miles with my parents and siblings. As a toddler, in 1957, we lived in Tanana, Alaska, on the Yukon River, where my physician father was stationed with Public Health, as the primary physician for the region. Then, we kids were carted off to Montana for a short stint before moving to Tulare, California. Here, my father worked in the Tulare County Hospital, where our family remained for a season; after which, like geese in the spring, we migrated back to Alaska in July 1961.

In the town of Soldotna (Sol-DOT-nah), my father joined the itinerant physician, Dr. Paul Isaak. Soldotna was hardly a proper town, not much more than a gravel intersection of two roads connecting other small communities. Soldotna's 500 inhabitants were scattered on homesteads of various sizes. Few inhabitants, yes, but with the Swanson River oil discovery in 1957, young families had headed to this north country for work, and the community needed more than a once-or-twice-a-week family doctor. While I had a patchwork of memories of those previous locations, the homestead would anchor who and what I was to become.

For me, the main attractions in Soldotna were Vera's Variety Store and Wilson's Grocery. Wilson's was a stone's throw from our first in-town house and Vera's was just beyond Wilson's. At Vera's, I poked around what appeared to be an endless inventory of model airplanes, both plastic and balsa wood. She may have had other things on the tightly packed shelves, but I never made it past the airplanes. Yes, Vera knew how to generate sales. If one of the models did not claim my dime or quarter, the candy rack on the way out would. Even if I made it out of Vera's with a nickel, I had to walk past Wilson's, where there was more candy.

Six months later, when we moved nearer Dad's clinic, Derk's Trading Post was a short distance away, and even though heavy trucks traveled intermittently on the rough and dusty road, Mom let me walk over to explore his larger collection of plastic model airplane kits and Matchbox vehicles. Mom appreciated other in-town amenities, such as two grocery stores, a day-old bakery—even though she baked most of our bread—the knitting-fabric store, and the post office, since she wrote to her family at least twice a week. That was about it for conveniences.

When we moved out of the relative civilization of Soldotna in 1963 to the 80-acre homestead, I was seven-and-a-half. This acreage became known to our family as the Gaede (GAY-dee)-Eighty Homestead and later, on maps, as the Gaede-Eighty Subdivision.

On that final day in town, Dad adjusted his hat, which covered his wavy black hair, and climbed into the driver's seat of the split-pea-green 1961 VW micro-bus.

His slight build and average height revealed no clue of a rugged hunter, bush pilot, and homesteader. I had heard the stories and viewed the Kodak slides and the jumpy 8mm movies he had taken when he'd hunted polar bear in the Arctic and then survived an emergency landing in a blizzard along the Arctic coast in his puny fabric and steel-tube two-place Piper J-3. I'd watched him ceaselessly cut down tree after tree in a thick forest. Yes, he was thin. His parents had been poor farmers in Oklahoma and Kansas, and there was never enough to eat. Even now, he did not carry an extra ounce of weight. All the same, he was an Alaskan man.

Short, feminine, and strong, Mom slid open the side door to the rear seats and stood aside. She worked ably alongside her husband, whether moose hunting or building an enormous brush pile from the trees they had felled together. Indoors, she kept kindling in the tinder box by the woodstove, rhubarb pies baking, sourdough starter rising, and all four of us children cleaned and bathed—at least for Sunday church. With a touch of lipstick and soot-stained leather gloves, she was a homemaker, traditional wife, and Alaskan homesteader.

My three sisters and I piled into the back of the bus and fought for the window seats. Naomi, the eldest, age 13, attempted to establish some semblance of order. Her shoulder-length, brown-black hair flew to and fro as she shouted commands at her siblings. Perhaps she thought her new black-rimmed cat-eye glasses would grant her authority. Alas, that was not the case, and she soon gave up trying to be our traffic controller. Ruth, age 12, grabbed a seat. I wanted that spot and protested loudly. With a toss of her wavy brown hair, she resolutely refused to budge, a rock amidst the chaos. She was stubborn. She had to be, with an older sister, one brother, and a cute baby sister. Where did she fit into the mix?

Mishal, age five, with brown eyes sparkling and curly black hair bobbing, giggled and bounced like a ping pong ball from one spot to another. Attempts of management or intimidation eluded her.

With the brood satisfactorily caged in the back, Mom pulled the door shut and swung up onto the front bench seat. From where I sat, I could see the back of her head, her auburn hair tastefully corralled by a scarf. My mother was beautiful. Dad turned the key, the VW muttered to life, and we headed west. We joggled and rattled down gravelly, dusty Kalifonsky (Kal-eh-FON-skee) Beach Road (now known as Kalifornsky Beach Road) for two miles before veering left onto Gas Well Road. After an additional mile, we turned right onto another gravel road, which marked the south end of our homestead.

A couple hundred yards onto our property, we drove past our log cabin on the left, partially hidden by tall black spruce. Another hundred yards farther was the circle driveway to our homestead house, also on the left. Its bi-level design was popular during the 1960s. The convenient, although crowded ground-level entry pressured individuals to go up a short flight of stairs to the main rooms or down to the daylight basement. Naturally, congestion resulted, and often, children and adults found themselves pushed up or down onto one of the steps. On the other hand, the bottom step upwards enabled young and old to sit and put on boots and shoes. Unlike our previous houses, this one had two bathrooms.

Dad pulled up in front of the house, and we tumbled out.

Construction on the Gaede's Homestead House

This trip was not our first to the property. During the previous two years, trees were felled, stumps bulldozed, a pair of driveways prepared, a log cabin built, and finally, the homestead house raised. It was a family affair. Dad had subdued a portion of the wilderness with his chainsaw, while Mom, my two older sisters, and I worked with axes; although, I must admit, in my first attempt to take down a wimpy, rubbery spruce sapling, my small hatchet ricocheted off the thin trunk, sliced through my boot, and split my big toe. Mom promptly confiscated the hatchet. Dad, the doctor, pronounced the wound non-lethal and demoted me from axe-bearer to stick-carrier. This incident was not a promising start to my young homesteading life.

That was then. Today was different. Today, August 28, 1963, we moved in, albeit to an uncompleted house. There were no windowpanes in the basement, just the rough openings. Sawdust decorated our bedding, and mosquitoes flew in and out at will. At least the frost stayed outdoors. The plumbing in the house was not in, although a single hose delivered ice-cold water from our shallow well. A doorless outhouse offered an unrestricted view of the woods. The rough, plywood seat discouraged loitering, and mosquitoes eagerly exploited exposed skin. I learned that business should be conducted as quickly as possible.

I did not care about these crude conditions. I beheld the deep forest around me and inhaled the aromas of spruce, moss, berry bushes, and even a whiff of a woodstove fire wafting from another homesteader's cabin. We were now in *our* house.

Grandma Bertha and Grandpa Solomon Leppke (Lep-KEE) already occupied the cabin. Earlier in August, they had temporarily left their farm in Kansas to help their daughter, my mom, settle in on the homestead. Grandma was a solidly built woman, larger framed than my petite mother, yet like my mother, Grandma was organized and efficient. Despite being at the edge of the Alaska frontier, she insisted on keeping her gray hair neat and tidy. And she always wore a dress. And thick brown hosiery. And an apron. Grandpa was tall. A competent carpenter, his daily attire consisted of blue and white striped coveralls with a matching hat.

Bertha Leppke Assisting in Lowering a Septic Tank

Solomon Leppke Digging a Well with a Hand Auger

When I first met him, I tugged at Mom's coat sleeve and whispered, "Does he drive a train?" He reminded me of a locomotive engineer I had seen in one of my books.

Mom smiled and laughed. "No. He's a farmer. That's what he wears to keep his clothes underneath clean."

Well, even if he didn't drive trains, I liked him. His soft smile and deep, rumbly voice were a welcome counterpart to Grandma's sometimes gruff and abrupt manner.

Construction on the Gaede's Homestead Cabin

Bertha Leppke, Mishal, Mark, Ruth, and
Elmer in Front of the Gaede's Cabin

The cabin had a hand-dug well, a pitcher pump, and a sink that drained out the wall behind it into the backyard. Since that was more plumbing than in the house, we ate meals there. At suppertime, we kids ran a 50-yard dash ahead of Dad and Grandpa down the trail that snaked through the woods between the two dwellings.

"I can beat you!" shouted Naomi.

Ruth deliberately bumped into her. The single-track narrow trail crisscrossed with tree roots, and easily knocked her competitor off-balance.

Laughing, teasing, and trying to keep from falling into mossy trail-sides, we scrambled across the finish line, bounced up the cabin steps, kicked off our shoes on the porch, and swung open the heavy homemade slab door.

Behind the short counter, Grandma and Mom glanced up at our arrival, both clad in colorful homemade bib aprons.

"Go wash up," Mom said matter-of-factly.

Without further comment, she and Grandma put the finishing touches on the evening meal. The sound of sizzling grease and the smell of fried chicken filled the air.

I was not inclined to join the line in front of the metal wash basin on a low shelf next to the kitchen counter. I had already wiped my hands on the front of my shirt, and they looked clean to me.

With no stove or oven in the cabin, Mom and Grandma made simple yet stomach-warming meals prepared in an electric skillet, powered by an electrical cord trailing through the woods from the house, or over an open fire in front of the cabin. We looked forward to Mom's extra-crispy, mouth-watering fried moose minute steaks, although with her primitive cabin and outdoor kitchen, we missed the mashed potatoes that usually accompanied that menu. In the mornings, she made pancakes in the electric skillet.

As a child, these shared experiences of grandparents, siblings dashing through the woods on root-rutted paths, and swatting mosquitoes as we ate around the campfire simmered into fond family memories, not that I knew it then, but I would appreciate them years later.

Within two months, the house was closed in, and the plumbing was operational. A fireplace and an oil-burning furnace provided heat. No packed boxes remained. For the first time in my life, I had my own bedroom. Not with a sister! This enormous 9-by-10-foot bunker served as my base of operations for preparing and launching expeditions into the untamed wilderness of our 80 acres.

Cleared Area along the Road in Front of the Gaede's House

After Dad and Mom cut down trees on either side of the road in front of the house and cabin, the road served as an all-season airstrip, the kind local bush pilots used all the time. And the kind pilots accustomed to paved, marked, official runways would fly over and declare unserviceable. Down the center of the 80 acres, Mom and Dad had started cutting down trees for a longer, wider runway. Why? To "prove up." To actually own a homestead, a percentage of land had to be cleared and planted with a harvestable crop. Since the land had to be cleared anyway, laying it out as an airstrip was the obvious choice. The first year's crop was oats, which unfortunately molded in the wet fall weather. The next year we planted hay, which was better suited for the area, and it produced a ton an acre.

During the summer months, they put on hold the airstrip project. For one reason, completing the house was a top priority, and for another, they could not safely burn the branches from the felled trees during the summer months because of forest fire risks. Every decision had a logical reason.

Fifty-to-70-foot-tall black spruce filled the 600 feet between the front road and the runway, and tree stumps poked up from trees used for the log cabin. Moss, lowbush cranberry (lingonberry), blueberry, and crowberry plants covered the forest floor. Scattered here and there were patches of waist-high willows. "Waist-high" to me meant about 20 inches. This small, wooded area provided a safe area for me to roam. If I lost my sense of direction, I eventually ended up at a road or a clearing with which to orient myself. Neither I nor my parents were concerned about such things as moose or bears, although those critters were undoubtedly in the area. I soon learned to navigate myself using landmarks. As I chased squirrels and small birds, a fallen tree, a scored tree trunk, or a rare grassy patch became reference points. I also listened to the sound of saws and hammers, which told me where the house was, even if I could not see it.

Felled Trees on What Would Become Gaede Private Airstrip

The downed, limbed tree trunks on the partially cleared airstrip invited me to a challenging playground of narrow walkways. Dad had not yet gathered and stacked the bare logs, which lay scattered like so many pick-up sticks. I walked the trunks, starting at the large end and working my way to the narrow tip without falling off. Walking the ones angled on top of others was especially precarious since they bounced and wobbled when

I neared the end. What a perfect game for a boy. What a way to develop balance and coordination. I loved it! Despite all this wandering about, not once did I hear Mom call out frantically, "Mark, where are you!" She did not attempt to ride herd on us kids. Perhaps this nonchalance stemmed from her background as a farm girl when she and her siblings and cousins ran freely through fields and caught fish in streams; or, on the other hand, maybe she was absorbed with laundry, cooking meals, baking cinnamon rolls, splitting wood, stripping bark off felled trees, and futilely attempting to keep the wilderness outside her house, where it belonged. Possibly, like me, she just lost track of time.

Since it was fall, school was in session. During the first fall semester on the homestead, school buses didn't run down Gas Well Road. That meant my older sisters and I had to walk the mile to where Gas Well intersected Kalifonsky Beach Road. It was not uphill both ways. Still, at minus 30 degrees, it was a long way, especially since we had to depart in plenty of time to see the bus headlights piercing the darkness coming toward us rather than watching the glow of taillights moving away while we stood helplessly in the cold. However, the twice daily slog down Gas Well was part of homestead life and we took it in stride.

"Bundle up, children," Mom instructed us after breakfast as she finished wrapping bologna sandwiches for our lunchboxes.

All our winter gear, except our coats, was stashed in a large cardboard box in the main entryway closet.

"I can't find my muffler," Ruth said in frustration, searching for her wool scarf.

"Ruth, it's in the bottom of the box," Naomi, the coordinator, stated, then added,

"Mark, here's one of your mittens."

To our advantage, a door was not put on the closet for a number of years, so we did not have to battle opening and closing it while we thrashed about, struggling to find the outdoor gear that fit or belonged to us individually. From time to time, a free-for-all ensued.

For the most part, I did not have to compete for those resources since my mittens were smaller than my sisters'. My problem was deciding whether to wear warmer, wool ones that the snow stuck to or snow-resistant plastic-coated ones, which were colder. Sometimes, it just came down to which ones were dry.

When the temperature dipped close to minus 40 degrees, Mom or Dad drove us to the intersection. Granted, riding in the VW bus was only a marginal improvement since we had no garage, and it sat in the front yard with an extension cord running up under the hood to provide power for the tank heater. The vehicle, or "Chariot," as Mom named it, sat cold and dark until someone started it; even then, the inside heating system lacked enthusiasm.

The school bus carried students who were in grades one to eight. There was no kindergarten. I was in second grade and got off with the rest of the kids at Soldotna Elementary School, before the bus continued to Kenai High School. Sometime after Christmas break, buses started running down Gas Well; then, the walk from our house was only 300 yards, albeit still in the dark, with twinkling stars overhead, in the pre-dawn, when the sun didn't clear the horizon until 10:30 a.m., after which it sleepily made a mere appearance before laying its head back to rest by 3 p.m.

"Watch out for moose," Mom called after us as we shuffled down our unplowed driveway and the road to Gas Well Road with our metal lunch boxes beating a muted cadence against our snow pants. She did not say this with urgency, but more like, "Goodbye, have a good day at school." "We will," we said in unison, not that we would be able to see one of the

13

brown giants until we bumped into it. There were no streetlights. But in November, Mom strung Christmas lights around the inside frame of our floor-to-ceiling living room window, and like a light-house beacon, those colorful lights glittering through the trees guided us home.

Riding the bus introduced me to other kids. Since we all lived on homesteads and not on a city block with houses next to each other, we did not regularly encounter kids outside our family except at church or school. The Herr boys, George (nine) and Jimmy (seven) walked up the road from their family's adjacent homestead, and we shared the same bus stop. The bus then stopped at the end of other driveways; accordingly, I learned where some of my classmates lived. The Kraxberger twins, Rick and Scott, who were my age, and their brother, Randy, who was several years older, lived only a quarter mile away. Across the road from them, Dwight Ross, also my age, emerged. I recognized some of these kids from when we had lived in town. Now, they were my neighbors.

I was not the most outgoing kid. As the bus rumbled along, I sat silently and observed the interaction around me. The students established a pecking order, and I quickly surmised that I was on the bottom tier given my size. I shifted uncomfortably in my seat and willed myself to be invisible. Maybe I would start growing soon.

With the onset of winter, outdoor construction slowed to a halt. Grandma and Grandpa had returned to Kansas, and without those two worker bees, some of the energy to complete projects departed with them. Even though the house was livable, the basement floor remained bare concrete. Dad made the most of what could have been an inconvenience. He painted a shuffleboard layout at either end of the hallway. Upstairs, except for the kitchen and bathroom linoleum, he did not camouflage the unfinished plywood—for years. I did not mind, although I think Mom got tired of mending the holes in my socks, holes that innocently resulted from Mishal and me racing around the living room and sliding on the plywood floors.

It was not as though I ran around the house unconstrained by Mom or climbed the walls with restless energy. Before the daylight hours got too short and the snow too deep, I burned off or froze off excess energy with Dad on Saturdays, when he typically went out to cut down more trees. I admired this man, my father. He was rugged. I wanted to be like him and have his approval, too. He did not sleep in late on Saturdays, however, so if I wanted to be with him, I had to get up and get going.

The soft sound of the radio on the kitchen table drifted down to my bedroom, and I knew Mom and Dad were up. I could smell toast. Maybe Dad was already out the door! I threw on some clothes, flew out of my room, and bounded up the stairs. When I saw Dad still at the table, I momentarily relaxed. But just because he was at the table did not mean he hadn't finished eating and was ready to head out the door. As a doctor, he was always one phone call away from a trip back into town to handle an emergency or deliver a baby, and he inhaled his food.

"Dad, I'm almost ready. Wait for me!" I said urgently.

He glanced up.

"It's okay, Mark. Go ahead and eat while I read the *Daily Bread* devotional for you and Mom."

He slid a box of Corn Flakes in my direction.

I was not too late after all.

Mom set a bowl and spoon down in front of me and put a plate with homemade molasses bread toast next to the bowl.

I hastily dumped flakes in the bowl and added pale-blue powdered milk, followed by a heaping teaspoon of sugar. Dad read out loud the devotional while I gulped the cereal and swallowed some reconstituted canned orange juice.

By the time I had polished off my breakfast, Dad was already down at the entry landing, filling his green Army surplus coat with supplies. He stuffed folded newspaper and matches to start a fire in an upper pocket. In another, he stashed an extra pair of double-thumbed wool gloves. Another pouch held a flashlight. Outfitting himself before leaving the house was *his* self-prescribed chore. I had another. Felling tall spruce trees, chopping off branches, and tossing the debris into a fire while wading through deep snow, was exerting, and my daddy would get thirsty. Here is where I was an important player. Even though I had lost my job as a hatchet boy, Mom and Dad gave me another job, that of water boy.

"Here, Mark," said Mom from the top of the stairs. "Take this water."

I cautiously reached for the cleaned and water-filled Miracle Whip quart jar.

I knew Dad would take a break during our work and drink deeply from the jar. "Thanks, Mark," he would say. And I appreciated his approval.

We walked the same route to the work site and as the snow deepened, the trail became a narrow groove, with snow mounting higher and higher on either side. "Too deep" for Dad and "too deep" for me were two different matters. If I would fall out of the groove and plunge into the powdery topography, I might not be found until springtime!

In these shared experiences, I did my best to prove I was a good homestead boy. Sometimes, I succeeded; other times, my efforts literally fell short. Take, for instance, when I attempted a simple task, such as cleaning up an area after he had limbed a fallen tree with his axe. I planned to latch onto some smaller branches, drag them toward the fire, and fling them onto the burning pile. Try as I would, before I got within range, I felt the blaze scorch my cheeks, and I'd have to retreat. I glanced over at Dad. Did he see my failed attempt? Was he disappointed in me? Maybe not. He kept working. I gathered my strength, took a deep breath, hurled the branch as hard as possible, and prayed it to land in the fire. I repeated this pattern over and over, then sighed in resignation and settled for just being close to the target zone. Despite my inefficiency, being outside with my dad was the best part of the day. Gratefully, he never criticized my shortcomings. "There you go," he would say to encourage me when one of my branches landed in the fire.

Elmer Working in the Woods

Even when the snow started or the temperature dropped, Dad worked steadily. He appeared to have unlimited fortitude. Indeed, more than mine. Did the severe cold cause his nostrils to contract, like mine did? I wondered. Did frost nibble at his fingers? I watched him chop tree limbs rhythmically and listened to the fire snap with new tinder tossed onto it. I noticed the sparks flying onto his olive-green parka and burning little dark spots. After what seemed like ages, he stoked the fire one more time and announced, "That's it!" And in snow-subdued silence and disappearing dusk, we headed back to the house.

This weekend ritual went on until February when the snow was waist-high to Dad, too deep for even him to walk through anymore. And then I would have survived what had seemed like walking in the bottom of a white canyon.

CHAPTER 2

THE LONG WINTER'S NIGHT

WHEN OUTDOOR ACTIVITY CEASED altogether, we settled down in the house for winter; winter, when eventually daylight hours would narrow from 10:30 a.m. to 2:30 p.m., and even then, the sun did not have the energy to climb over the treetops. On cloudy days, the hours would pass through a quiet dusk before returning to darkness. There was school during the week and church on Sunday mornings, Sunday evenings, and Wednesday nights. On those rare moments when I roamed restlessly around the house, I learned the hard way not to announce to Mom, "I'm bored." She had a list. She could assign chores to me.

"Go clean your room," she instructed me. Evidently, her opinion of *clean* differed from mine because I thought my room was already in good order.

"Pick up your toys" was also on her list. That one was particularly annoying since I had my toys strategically placed where I could find them later.

Fortunately, I was a curious kid, and fortunately, Dad had invested in a set of World Book Encyclopedias. I spent hours lying on my stomach on the concrete floor in the basement, reading those works of knowledge. I preferred pictures over text and found the "A" volume with "Aircraft" and the "S" volume with "Snakes" particularly fascinating. Even our Webster's Dictionary intrigued me. "Why are there so many words?" "And how can one word have so many different meanings?" I also ordered books through school and started a small library in my bedroom. The first book, *Yellow Eyes*, was about a mountain lion kitten growing up. Reading exercised my mind and helped me deal with so much time indoors.

Gaede Family Singers: (bk.) Mishal, Ruby, Elmer, Ruth (ft.) Naomi, Mark

Another activity was music. Mom and Dad grew up on the farm without much entertainment, not that they had time to spare. What time they squeezed out, they often spent with family or relatives playing music. Consequently, when our family moved to Soldotna, Mom and Dad compiled a collection of hymns, choruses, and Scripture readings, and we traveled to local churches and performed these as a family.

Our instruments had to be portable and fit in our VW bus with our family of six. Mom played piano by ear, but lugging around a piano was obviously not possible. Dad asked ahead of time if a specific church had a piano; if not, he and Mom came up with other alternatives. We could take along our collapsible pump organ and she would play that, or Dad could play his accordion. Mom was a multi-talented musician and also played a mandolin. To add to our orchestra, Naomi strummed a ukulele and Ruth played accordion. I also had an accordion, though it was about the size a cute little circus monkey would play.

Our small group sang in harmony: Dad sang tenor, Mom alto, and we children sang melody. Mishal was still discovering her musical abilities and provided impromptu choreography as she rocked back and forth to the rhythm of the music. This embarrassed our stoic parents of Mennonite heritage, yet she was the most entertaining and got more smiles and laughs than the rest of us, especially my other two sisters, who never smiled while on stage.

My parents, particularly my mother, bequeathed me with a musical gene, most likely coming from Grandma (Litke) Leppke's side of the family. My past exposure to music gave me an excellent sense of pitch. As a toddler, I had listened to children's music on a small phonograph Mom and Dad had purchased for us kids. As a preschooler, during our short stint in California, I had curled up on the couch in the evenings and listened in rapt fascination to *Tchaikovsky's Nutcracker Suite* coming from our new Hi-Fi system. The song *Dance of the Sugar Plum Fairy* was so happy, but the one about the *In the Hall of the Mountain King* was scary! During the day, I heard the sounds of the high school band across the street through our open windows, and I would pitch-match some of the notes on our portable pump organ. Finding the matching pitch was like a game, and I developed a knack for doing so. Weaving together all this musical background were the close-knit harmonies of the congregational singing and choirs at the Mennonite Brethren Church we attended.

Before my sixth birthday, I started with the tiny accordion. My strong sense of pitch, however, led to complications when playing with our family ensemble. There were only a few buttons for the bass, which meant I was limited to playing in the keys of C, F, and G, and I could not play any minor chords. I immediately noticed this and frowned when our family rehearsed if I could not play the right bass notes. Given my diminutive stature, purchasing a more advanced accordion was out of the question. But it did not stop me from sneaking Ruth's accordion when no one was around and finding the *right* bass notes. As it turned out, given my dissatisfaction with the "monkey accordion," I was handed a second mandolin and soon enjoyed playing mandolin duets with Mom.

My formal music education started in 1962 when I was six-and-a-half, and we still lived in town. Mom and Dad found someone who offered piano lessons. At first, I was intrigued by basic music theory. I easily learned the names of the lines and spaces in both musical clefs and the duration values of each type of note. Nevertheless, I soon became bored with the simple songs I was supposed to learn. I also had strong preferences. I worked on the songs I liked and neglected the ones I did not care for.

Over the next several years, my lessons continued in starts and stops as music teachers came and went. By the time I progressed to more advanced music, my *ears* overruled my *eyes*, and I ended up playing songs the way I thought they should sound, not by the written notes. This tendency caused considerable consternation among my various piano teachers. I also developed a fear of music lessons when one particular music teacher slapped my hands whenever I made a mistake. By fourth grade, I was so stressed by music lessons I made up excuses to get out of them. That was when Mom and Dad pulled the plug on my lessons. Despite those negative experiences, my passion for music grew relentlessly for the rest of my life.

I also spent winter months working on model airplanes. I saved the allowance we kids earned by cleaning Dad's clinic and bought small plastic model kits, glue, paint, and paint brushes from Vera's Variety or Derk's Trading Post.

As an inquisitive kid, I discovered that not all glue was the same. There was glue for wooden models, glue for plastic models, and then there was Elmer's glue. Initially, I reasoned that Elmer's glue was named after my dad and therefore would work on anything, maybe even people. After all, when it dried on my fingers, it peeled off like skin. However, after some experimentation, I found that material-specific glue worked the best and that Dad's Elmer's glue was to be used on arts and crafts, not serious projects like model airplanes.

I assembled most of the kits without looking at the instructions. After all, how hard could it be? There were wings, a fuselage, some tailpieces, and landing gear. Most of the time, I ended up with pieces left over. This result was actually okay since they were unnecessary, and I had learned from Dad that an airplane needed to be as light as possible. Therefore, leaving those parts out was an improvement and I kept a box of "spares." Using thread from Mom's sewing box, I suspended the completed airplanes from my bedroom ceiling. A thumbtack secured the string to the ceiling tile. I was particularly interested in WWII aircraft from both sides of the war and soon had aerial battles staged above my bed.

I did not play much with my siblings. To start with, they were girls, and girls had cooties. I learned this fact at recess in first grade. At recess. And, therefore a fact. Also, Naomi and Ruth were so much older than me that we lived in different universes. Admittedly, Ruth entered into my universe when she and I collaborated musically. She would play our newly acquired electronic organ, and I would play our piano. Or we would switch instruments, depending on the song. This pleasure offered another option for winter hibernation.

My relationship with Mishal was more adversarial and probably heightened in winter when we were cooped up in the house. She and I became sparring partners early on. Sometimes literally. The constant verbal back and forth exasperated Mom and Dad.

"Will you two quit bickering?" Mom said repeatedly. Or sometimes it was:

"Go outside, you two!" This later admonition was not realistic in winter until Dad installed a tall yard light. Even then, the threat of going out into the winter night felt like banishment and sometimes called for a shaky, temporary truce.

Occasionally, Mishal unintentionally crippled one of my model airplanes, which I had parked on the couch. These accidents ignited my irritation. After hours of pretending to fly my airplanes through the mountains and shooting landings on remote bush airstrips, such as the couch or coffee table, I would leave it there momentarily. When I returned, I would find it lying on its side with a broken landing gear or wing. Why hadn't my sister checked with the control tower before descending on the couch?

"Mom, Mishal broke another one of my airplanes again," I wailed.

"I did not!" objected my little sister hotly.

"Did so!"

"Did not!"

Those exchanges were not only in winter, with the excuse of close quarters.

One summer, our back-and-forth became physical. Tall fireweed stalks became swords. Of course, these flimsy stems were harmless. Then, our intent to aggravate the other escalated to willow whips, which were heavier and did not break. All was well until Mishal caught me across the cheek with one swipe. That detonated my temper, and I gave in to yelling and name-calling. Mishal made a beeline up the back steps and down into the bedroom she shared with Ruth. Doors banged everywhere.

Mishal by the Rabbit Hutches

In all fairness, I might have had a part in the ongoing testiness between us. Perhaps she still held against me the incident with the rabbit. Sometimes, things just happen. Given I was anything but muscular, the surprise was as much mine as anyone else's. As mentioned earlier, Mom and Dad had been farmers. Farmers have animals. Like other homesteads in the area, our homestead was like a farm. At one time or another, we had chickens, ducks, geese, sheep, goats, horses, and rabbits. Except for the horses, these animals were primarily food animals, whether for eggs, milk, or meat. They were not pets. Our pets were dogs and cats. All the same, that did not prevent Mishal and me from adopting and naming two rabbits. Hers was a charcoal and white bunny named Pepper. Mine was a butterscotch and white one named Salt. These animals were caged at night to protect them from stray dogs or a rare coyote. During the day, we carried them around and often let them loose in the yard. They were tame.

One evening, after we had played with them, Mom called us in for supper. She asked me to catch the two non-pets and put them in their cages for the night. Mishal skipped toward the house with a smirk on her face. I caught Salt easily enough, but Pepper kept hopping out of reach. Again, my temper reared its head. Why me? Why not Mishal? I reached down, grabbed a silver-dollar-sized stone, wound up, and threw it hard toward Pepper, who was still nibbling grass about 25 feet away.

To my horror, the rock flew straight and true and smacked Pepper in the back of the head. The rabbit flopped over and lay still. I stood paralyzed, hoping and praying it would rouse and hop off. Slowly, I walked over and nudged it with my foot. No response. I looked around furtively. No one was watching. I picked up the now-deceased bunny, carried it to its cage, opened the door, and placed it inside, arranging it to look as if it were sleeping.

Not unexpectedly, it was still in that position when Mishal went out to check on it in the morning. She jumped to the immediate and correct conclusion that I had something to do with its demise. I offered her Salt as restitution. This exchange did not placate her. I doubt it was any consolation when Salt ended up on the supper table, butchered, dipped in egg, flour, and fried. Tasty.

I'm sure more than once Mom pondered, while kneading bread, how her expectations had gone wrong. She and Dad had decided to adopt a baby to be my companion, just like Naomi and Ruth were companions who played so nicely together. I would not hear the details until later about Mishal's birth at the Public Health Hospital in Tanana, along the Yukon River, and her mother wanting our family to include her child in our family. I just thought it was pretty cool to have an Eskimo sister—and even if I fought with her, I'd dare anyone else to say anything unkind about her or the Native people.

To Alaskans, the term "breakup" is not about relationships, although relationships may indeed be tested during the long winter months. No, breakup happens when the lengthening days and strengthening sunlight in March herald the retreat of winter. Breakup is when river ice begins to melt, break up, and is carried downstream. It is also when dirt roads break up and become muddy bogs, bringing travel across them to a halt.

During breakup, exploring the homestead again became possible for me. On frosty mornings, the crusty snow held my weight and allowed me to scamper anywhere I wanted, although I had to be back near the house before it warmed up enough for me to break through. As breakup progressed, water puddles, ice, and mud slowly replaced the snow. The near-sterile scent of winter was exchanged for occasional whiffs of gas, now released from decaying plants trapped in the frozen ground. Along the edge of the runway, this mixture of snow, ice, mud, and water became an enticing challenge to traverse in my knee-high rubber boots. I jumped from ice patch to ice patch as I navigated this maze, pretending to hunt polar bears on ice floes as my dad had. A few times, I misjudged the stability or thickness of the ice and ended up with icy water pouring into my boots.

That called for a hasty retreat through the woods and back to the house.

I banged through the front door and shouted, half-crying, "Mom, Mom! I fell through the ice! My feet are freezing and I'm cold!"

"Go find dry socks, Mark," she said sympathetically. "I will make hot cocoa."

The hot cocoa chased the chill away and sitting in the kitchen with Mom, watching her shape cinnamon rolls and answering her questions about my outdoor discoveries, recharged my spirits. She loved the outdoors as much as I did and enjoyed hearing the tales of my explorations.

Even when the snow was almost entirely gone, the ground remained frozen, and puddles persisted, some quite large. I had spied insects starting to appear in them and subsequently needed to investigate the situation. I could see little water-boatman beetles beneath the surface while "skaters" skimmed across the top. My short knee-high boots proved insufficient for in-depth examination, and on more than one occasion, I approached Mom and Dad for an upgrade in foot gear.

"Do you think you could buy me a pair of hip boots?" I asked wistfully.

"Not right now," Mom and Dad responded.

Their identical response suggested they were in cahoots. I suspect they had several reasons for denying what seemed to me a reasonable request. Mom probably thought that I would drown myself by getting too adventuresome. Dad likely looked at my short legs and figured hip boots wouldn't gain me much. It was probably because they didn't make hip boots that small.

Despite this equipment handicap, I occasionally captured some of the puddle dwellers with a strainer borrowed from the kitchen and transferred them via a glass jar to our newly acquired aquarium, where I could watch them in a more controlled environment. I discovered that water-boatmen got along fine with guppies and neon tropical fish. However, the larger water beetles would devour the baby guppies. Sad, but still fascinating.

When breakup had passed, the runway was once again open to airplanes. Or, in my case, pretend airplanes. I was nine when Dad purchased a used Honda 90 Trail bike from one of the local schoolteachers. I'm sure they discussed top speed before the sale was agreed upon. It was slow. My bike was faster. But the Honda had a motor. This motorized vehicle became even more fun when I discovered it had two rear sprockets, and switching the chain to the smaller one almost doubled the top speed from 20 mph to 35 mph. I had a vivid imagination, and one of my favorite pastimes was to hop on my Honda and pretend I was a WWII fighter pilot. I had read about these pilots and built models of most of their aircraft. I knew the model numbers, top speeds, and service ceilings of these daring planes. I was also well-acquainted with basic WWII fighter tactics.

One day, I strapped on my helmet firmly, started my motorbike, and entered my fighter pilot mode. I firewalled the throttle of my P-51D Mustang, and the 2000-horsepower Rolls-Royce engine hurtled me into the air. Heading down the driveway, I searched the skies for the enemy. Instantly, I spotted an ME-109 on the road in front of our house. It spied me, banked steeply, and headed in my direction. He wanted to go head-to-head! Fine with me. He closed in. I armed my guns by flipping the high-low beam switch with my thumb. Tat-tat-tat-tat! My .50-caliber machine guns spit fire and lead. He flashed by my left wing. I nailed the brake, and the tail of my Mustang came around in a cloud of dust. A quick downshift, back on the throttle, and I was in pursuit. Where had he gone? Aha! There he was, doing lazy 360s around our circle driveway. I waited for him to pass, then eased onto his tail and closed in! Tat-tat-tat-tat! Smoke billowed from the 109. I saw the pilot eject as the stricken plane nosed over. Another one down!

I headed to the back runway to find more prey, maybe a Focke-Wulf 190 or another ME-109. Sure enough. They were everywhere. It didn't take long to clear the skies over Europe, and a few minutes later, I headed back to the hangar.

Halfway down the taxiway, my destination in sight, disaster struck. A yellowjacket flew inside my helmet, got trapped, and buzzed in my hair! "Mayday! Mayday!" I bailed off the Mustang, hit the ground rolling, and tore the helmet from my head. The yellowjacket flew off, and I stood momentarily, thanking God I was still alive. Then, I limped over to where the Mustang had crashed, lying on its side, the rear wheel still spinning. Wrestling it upright, I gingerly climbed back on and taxied to the hangar. I powered down the mighty Mustang and reviewed the day's mission on the way to my quarters.

Pushing the door open, I yelled, "Mom, when's supper?"

As the rabbit episode had illustrated, I sometimes let my temper get the best of me as a kid. When we first moved to Soldotna, we lived temporarily in a small house where the Soldotna Fire Station now stands. I forget what set me off but evidently Mom told me "No," probably to a cookie request or something equally important to a six-year-old. Whatever the reason, I angrily yanked the cord of an electric clock that was on a tall cabinet in the living room. The clock went flying and smashed into the floor, where it shattered. I gulped and stared at the carnage. Mom took a deep breath and then said quietly, "Wait until YOUR daddy comes home."

I was bright enough to comprehend that "*your daddy*" was not someone new to our household. I just had never heard it said quite like that before. It obviously meant that the seriousness of my offense had been handed to a higher court, kind of like hearing Mom say "Mark Anthony" instead of just "Mark," the former usually announced with increased intensity.

The rest of the day dragged on as I contemplated my doom. Not that I could tell time if I had wanted to. The time-keeping instrument was now history. Most days I was eager to see Dad walk up the dirt path to the front door. This would not be one of those days. Perhaps Mom would forget to tell Dad what had happened. Perhaps Dad would not care about the clock. But then I would glance up at the gaping vacancy on the top of the cabinet and know *that* was not going to happen.

First, I heard the mutter of the VW bus. Then, I heard Dad stomping the dirt off his feet outside the door. I wanted to run and hide, but the house was so small I did not have a bedroom, and I slept on the couch in the tiny living room. Maybe I could slip out the back door to Vera's Variety store, next door, where my older sisters were. Then, Dad opened the door and greeted Mom, who was instantly in front of him. I crouched on the floor, reorganized a set of farm animals, and willed myself invisible. Mom and Dad walked into the kitchen and talked in barely audible tones. When they finished, Dad walked into the living room, pointed to Naomi and Ruth's bedroom, and said, "We need to talk."

So much for being invisible. I nodded and followed him into the bedroom. He closed the door.

"Mom says you got angry and broke the clock. Is that correct?"

I glanced up. There was no smile on his face. I averted my eyes and nodded.

"Do you know that what you did was wrong?" he continued.

Oh, I surely knew it, all right. Like a deer in the headlights, I was stuck, my impending judgment bearing down on me. I knew I deserved a good thrashing. Tears crept into my eyes. "Yes," I whimpered.

"You know you deserve a spanking?"

I was sobbing now. Unable to speak, I nodded.

Dad was silent for a few seconds. Then he put his hand on my head and said, "I will not spank you this time, even though you deserve it."

What was this? I was guilty! I admitted it and had expected to pay the consequences. My tears were now tears of relief. After a minute or so, and with a damp shirt sleeve where I'd wiped my tears, I was able to pull myself together.

Dad opened the bedroom door, and we walked out. I stayed in the living room. He stuck his head in the kitchen and asked Mom when supper was. Then he backtracked to the hall closet, opened the door, and pulled out two fishing rods, and his tackle box. I was puzzled.

He looked at me and said, "Let's grab a pole and go fishing before supper."

Overjoyed, I pulled on my rubber boots and followed him out the door and across the gravel road to the Kenai River, so much in awe that he was *my daddy*.

It wasn't until years later that I realized how analogous this situation was to God showing His mercy and grace to all of us. While not a perfect parallel, Dad showed mercy by not giving me what I deserved. He then extended grace to me by taking me fishing and giving me something I did not deserve.

CHAPTER 3

EXPANDING
FRONTIERS

THE END OF SECOND GRADE MARKED the beginning
of my first full summer on the homestead, at which time my explorable
horizon expanded to Slikok (SLY-cock) Creek, one mile toward Soldotna.

"May I go to the creek, Mom?" I asked.

She had just finished running a damp rag along the clothesline behind
our house and had bent down to a laundry basket full of bedsheets. Neither
of us planned to waste a sunny day.

"Okay, but be careful," she replied.

I guess she figured I couldn't get into too much trouble without
hip boots.

I grabbed my jacket, called out a "Bye, Mom!" hopped on my single-
speed bike, and pedaled down dusty Gas Well Road. My parents had
forbidden me to ride the Honda off the homestead, and anyway, I could
pedal my bike almost as fast as the Honda could go. Sometimes, Mom was
complicit in my explorations and dropped me off at the creek on her way
into town. Today, she focused on household tasks.

At that time, Slikok Creek was a young boy's paradise. Slikok Creek winds through miles of swamp land before draining into the Kenai River. It has a gravelly base and spans 10 to 12 feet where it flows through a large culvert under Kalifonsky Beach Road at the intersection of Gas Well Road. Here the creek was a foot or two deep and not moving swiftly, so it was a relatively safe place to explore. Rainbow and Dolly Varden trout populated the creek. Salmon also spawned in it. Several old beaver dams created pools upstream, which were on private property and off-limits. In addition to the stream, three gravel pits were adjacent to it on the north side of Kalifonsky Beach Road. These had been excavated to provide material for the nearby roads. Since the water table in this area was shallow, those pits were filled with water. The two smaller rectangular pits were approximately 50 by 20 feet, with water only a couple feet deep. The largest pit was around 150 by 100 feet. The water at the western end was close to four feet deep, ramping up slowly to only a few inches deep on the eastern end. As summer progressed, these ponds became relatively warm.

I discarded my bike in the tall grass at the creek, kicked off my shoes, and waded into the knee-deep icy water. The rocks on the creek bottom felt rough beneath my feet. My curiosity and satisfaction superseded this discomfort, and I explored for a short time before scurrying up the bank and into the nearest pond to warm my cold, reddened legs in what felt like bath water.

Although I was usually on my own, I did not always have this location to myself. Two of the nearest neighbor boys occasionally played there, too. When this worked out, we scouted the area together. As we built friendships, we plotted these occurrences.

Mark with David Isaak on Gaede Private Airstrip

Not all friendships were with immediate neighbors. Take, for instance, David Isaak. David's father, Dr. Paul Isaak, was my father's business partner, and our families had much in common. Both fathers were physicians, they lived on homesteads, flew airplanes, and hunted. David and his younger brother were close to my age, and the three Isaak girls were close to my older sisters' ages. David and I had met in school. He was built like me, which was of some consolation since most of the other boys at school were bigger, and some eyed me as a target for bullying. With David, I could relax and not be on guard. Looking back at pictures of the two of us, we could have been twins—the same height, blue eyes, and brown hair, although mine was curly. Even though our homesteads were several miles apart, we spent many days playing together. If school was in session, the buses made transportation easy. Outside of the school year transportation had to be arranged by our mothers.

Although the creek and the gravel pits were not connected, that did not prevent us boys from attempting to stock the ponds with fish we caught in the creek. We scooped up fingerling or slightly larger fish and transported them with buckets up over the steep creek bank and down into the ponds on the other side. Then, we monitored the results. We discovered that the transplants in the smaller ponds did not last very long, while the ones in the large pond seemed to survive well into the following winter. Of course, we did not understand what was going on. At our age, oxygen starvation due to lack of water, plants, or winterkill when the ponds froze solid, was beyond our knowledge or understanding. It was educational, nonetheless.

Numerous frogs lived around the ponds as well. We could hear them calling.

"David, listen," I whispered. "Let's go find them."

Off we went with lidded glass jars in hand and stalked them in the grass and short reeds that grew along the shoreline. Most of the small amphibians escaped into the deeper water, but we managed to capture a couple now and then and take them home.

I built a terrarium of sorts for these creatures. It consisted of a galvanized tub lined with dirt, grass, sticks, a bowl of water, and a wire mesh cover. I parked this tub in my bedroom and caught flies to feed the frogs. Sometimes, the frogs escaped. I searched but never found one hiding in a corner, nor did I ever find frog mummies. Maybe Ruth's cats ate them.

Along with the fish and frogs, there were feathers, too. The bank between the creek and the gravel pits was home to cliff swallows. Captivated, I watched the graceful birds swoop across the sky and then unerringly disappear into holes in the bank. I wondered how they kept track of who belonged in which hole. It became my mission to catch one of these birds for closer examination. With much effort and persistence, I managed to scale the bank and peer into the holes. I told Mom later, "I could see them! They looked me in the eye!" Whereas I failed to capture a bird the first summer, later I did and was spellbound by how sleek and pretty it was. Then, having achieved my goal, I felt regret having caught it and turned it loose to be free. No doubt I traumatized it for life.

In those early years on the homestead, the creek and the watery gravel pits remained a significant gathering place for us neighborhood boys. One warm summer day, I pedaled to the creek and discovered a "naval battle" in the big pond. Turns out, the three Kraxberger boys were more innovative than I was when exploiting the possibilities. Perhaps their ability to conjure up such roughhouse plans stemmed from being in a family primarily of brothers. Although they did have one sister who was Mishal's friend.

The Kraxbergers had a well-drilling business and between all the trucks and other equipment, they had plenty of inner tubes. The boys kept theirs, along with an extra one or two, hidden in the brush along the pond shoreline.

The large inner tubes served as platforms for the conflict. Even though the water was not very deep the additional floatation provided the combatant a reprieve from the cool water or the ability to maneuver out of range to regroup and plot his next attack.

The battles started innocently enough. The boys floated on their backs in the tubes and paddled with their hands. The banter was good-natured. Before long, though, someone would splash the nearest boy; not much, just enough to get his attention. Then, another boy would send a wallop of water at the nearest sailor.

"Hey, watch it!"

"You watch it!"

"You trying to start something?"

"Hey, Mark. Grab a tube and come on out!"

That recruitment came from Scotty.

The volume of yelling, taunting, and laughing increased with the intensity of the skirmish. We hastily formed alliances, drew up battle lines, and designated targets.

We understood the rules. Ammunition could be nearly anything except sticks or rocks. We snickered at the suggestion of water guns. The weapon of choice was usually the muck on the bottom of the pond. The combatants felt along the bottom with their toes, scooped up mud and pond weed with their feet, reached into the water, grabbed this ammunition with their hands, and looked for an opponent to target. With some practice, a kid could gather "ammo" undetected while plotting his next salvo.

Chaos escalated. Before long, most of the warring parties displayed battle damage. No one rinsed off mud during hostile action, and if an opponent stayed in the fray after taking a hit, he displayed the muck as a badge of honor. If an opportunity arose, alliances might change mid-battle. This lack of loyalty resulted in objections and howls of protest, and the traitor finding himself battered by everyone. From time to time, the action wound down due to mud in an eye, which, unlike the Bible story of Jesus using mud to heal a blind man's sight, didn't heal anything. Sometimes, an adult showed up to tell the sailors it was time for supper. Reluctantly, we sloshed onto the bank. The adult frequently redirected one or all of us back into the water to rinse off muck and weeds from our T-shirts or hair, before we pedaled back home. All in all, we went our ways on friendly terms.

Not all the interaction at the creek was friendly. For whatever reason, some boys struggled to remain civil. One particularly sunny day, Mom dropped David and me down at the creek. We waded in the stream, caught small trout with our fishing lines, and generally took in the pleasures of outdoor living. At some point, two slightly older and larger boys showed up.

I nudged David and motioned to the ponds. So as not to act scared, we wandered nonchalantly over to the warmer waters. Before long, the boys followed. We continued to mind our own business and gave them a wide berth.

Then, soft dirt clods landed at our feet. Though not as widely known as the Geneva Convention, the undocumented "Homestead Convention" guidelines allowed dirt clods—but not rocks. David and I took refuge behind a mound of gravel. The other two hid behind another mound about 30 feet away. David and I were not big kids, yet we had good eye-hand coordination, and throwing dirt clods was a piece of cake. The older boys threw clods at us when we fetched more ammunition or otherwise showed up in their line of sight. David and I, conversely, lobbed our rounds over their bunker wall, even though we couldn't see them. Visible or not, we could tell our rounds were effective by the sound of their yells.

As our effectiveness increased, so did our opponents' frustration and anger. After a few minutes of unequal back and forth, we noticed rocks, not dirt clods, landing in our direction. Evidently, our opponents didn't recognize this "convention." I felt a pinch of fear with this escalation. The hair on the back of my neck began to rise. Given my size, I knew that outright physical conflict with larger adversaries would not end well. In retrospect, I could have used older brothers to teach me fighting skills. What I did have were fast, albeit short, legs. Thus, David and I abandoned our position, zig-zagged over the bank, down to the creek, and then across the road—with the two other boys in hot pursuit, briefly pausing to grab more stones. When we crossed the road and slid down the other side, we disappeared from their sight. Rather than stop at the creek edge, we hurried into the deep grass and hid. The boys crested the road and searched the creek bank.

After what seemed like hours, Mom showed up in the VW bus. She stopped above the culvert, opened the sliding side door, and called for me. David and I broke concealment and scrambled up the steep road bank. Breathlessly, we jumped through the open, sliding side door. Behind us, I could hear the boys shouting as they sighted us again.

"Mom! Mom! Go!" I screamed.

Mom hesitated. Frowning slightly, she asked, "Mark, what is wrong? What…?"

A rock flew through the open door and smacked the inside wall of the VW. Then, Mom saw the two boys winding up for another round. She threw the VW into gear and spun down the road toward town. I don't recall when we pulled the door shut.

After a minute or so of silence, she spoke, "I don't want you ever playing with those boys again…do you understand?"

I understood, and not just because she was telling me so.

In early winter, when temperatures dropped below freezing, the ponds glazed over. The shallow ponds provided a safe setting to test how thick ice had to be to support the weight of small kids on ice skates. I recall that an inch was workable if I didn't jump, but I was small and light. Two inches was the best thickness, pliable but not thick enough to develop big cracks. Wide cracks waited to grab our skate blades, bringing our skating to an abrupt and dramatic halt. The worst consequences of exceeding the weight limits of thinner ice would have been breaking through, soaking ourselves halfway to our waists, and calling it quits for the day.

Another time, I learned that if I kicked a hole in the thin ice and stood beside it, water would flow up and onto the ice. This effect became more pronounced when I called a friend to show him what I had discovered.

More water flowed out as more weight gathered around the hole, and the ice began to sink under the added weight. Even as grade school boys, we decided this was not a wise idea and skated off to drier ice.

I fell through the ice once, along the shallow edge. I escaped with only wounded dignity and wet feet. The behavior of ice, weight, and resulting overflow was something I remembered when I started spending more time flying with Dad.

An adult was often on-site for ice skating. Mom was the adult of choice since she loved nothing better than making a campfire, even if it was not for roasting hot dogs or marshmallows. When we kids felt the bite of cold on our cheeks or our fingers turning numb, we headed toward the smell of the wood fire and the sight of flames jumping merrily on the shoreline.

The frozen creek had a different character from the ponds. The flowing water required colder temperatures to freeze, and once it did, it was like a flat bobsled run. The course wove back and forth between three-foot-high banks, cushioned with thick, dead grass. Late-run coho salmon could be seen beneath the ice if the creek froze early enough. The fish had turned dark maroon by then, accented with yellow-white where their fins were slowly rotting.

"There's a big one!" someone would yell when he spotted a fish through the glass-like ice. That would bring the rest of us skating madly, blades flashing and ice chips flying to join the spotter. We viewed with amusement the salmon zipping along under the ice as we spooked them when we glided by on our skates.

If the snow held off long enough, the creek would continue to drop, and the ice would settle. It was flexible enough to stay attached to the bank and droop in the middle, creating areas like a half-pipe, and others as gently banked curves. With the wind blowing against our faces and our adrenaline at high pitch, we skated down the course as fast as we could. The conditions changed from day to day. The water level in the creek continued to drop since there was no rain to maintain the creek level. Once the creek dropped far enough or the ice got thicker, the ice fractured, and our smooth skating disappeared.

No two winters were the same. Sometimes, the snow came early and weighted down the thin ice, causing overflow. This prevented the ice from freezing smoothly and ruined the opportunities for ice skating on the ponds.

The onset of winter snows presented other prospects for outdoor fun. By the second winter, I knew the neighborhood boys better, and we often planned after-school homestead activities while riding the bus. Even though we were all just 9 to 12 years old, our households had acquired what kids on homesteads identified as essential: a snowmobile, or what Alaskans called snow machines. These were not the high-powered, liquid-cooled, fuel-injected, full-suspension, plush snow sleighs of today but were basic single-cylinder, air-cooled, carbureted, rough-riding, temperamental sleds. The low speed and questionable reliability kept us relatively safe and close to home. That was not to say that we did not find ways of coming home with new bruises or scraped cheeks. Falling off a towed sled at 30 mph could be plenty rough, depending on how hard the snow was.

Mark with Mishal on His Scorpion Snow Machine

My snow machine was significantly underpowered; attaining 30 mph was pure wishful thinking. Since I was only nine, perhaps Dad had purchased this one on purpose. It was difficult to start, too. When the engine was cold, the procedure was to unthread the single spark plug, squirt some starting fluid into the combustion chamber, reinstall the spark plug, set the choke to "full," disengage the "kill switch," say a quick prayer, and pull the starter rope. Sometimes, it just sputtered a bit then died. I would have to go through the tedious procedure all over again. Other times, I managed to keep the engine going long enough for it to warm up and stay running.

Another quirk was that the safety guard over the drive clutch and the pulley were prone to falling off. It was a nuisance to reinstall. At times, I gave up and left it off. One day, I hopped on the machine to make a trip down the runway. Just a casual spin. Suddenly, the rapidly spinning pulley grabbed a loose end of my woolen muffler. Bam! In one instant, it snapped my head down and snatched the muffler off my neck! I was extremely fortunate it did not pull my head into the pulley. The painful rope burn around my entire neck left me with a week-long reminder. After that, I never started a snow machine without the guard on.

One particularly entertaining group event was snow machine wars.

I pulled on my snowsuit and heavy winter boots, donned a wool hat and muffler, grabbed my mittens, and opened the front door to leave.

"I'm meeting Scott down at the Herrs'," I announced.

"What will you be doing?" Mom asked from the top of the split-level stairway.

"Snowmachining," I responded without providing additional details.

"Is your homework done?" she inquired. I found out later she had never completed high school, so our education was important to her.

"Yes, Mom," I said, in a respectful yet somewhat "of course" tone. I usually completed my homework in study hall at school.

"Okay, have fun," she replied.

My parents were outdoor enthusiasts, trusted us kids, and were comfortable with me spending time in my part of the Alaska frontier, which, at this point, only covered a mile or so from the house.

With that, I was out the door, walking down the driveway through the cone of light from the yard light and into the crisp darkness. I heard the other boys in the distance. I could distinguish voices when I neared the gathering, but that was about it.

"Who's coming tonight?" one asked.

"I think seven," came a response.

"I'm coming!" I yelled, still unseen in the blackness.

"Oh, hi, Mark," greeted Scott.

We picked sides, and the drivers mounted two snow machines. Behind each snow machine was an old car hood attached by a 15-foot rope. The non-drivers clambered aboard the hoods and loaded up with chunks of snow that served as ammo. Our battlefields were a pair of adjacent five-to-six-acre hayfields. The hay had been harvested in the fall, leaving a wide-open area to run the snow machines.

The designated drivers took off across the snowy fields, driving parallel to each other, while the fighters bounced along in the hoods and threw chunks of snow at each other. If the two hoods got close enough to bang into each other, it was fair game to try to unseat a member of the opposite team from their precarious perch and toss them overboard. Being so small, I did minimal tossing and, more often than not was the one tossed. Because it was dark, if a hood-rider was unseated, it might be a while before he was missed. Indeed, there were times when a driver looked back and found his command empty. A mix of voices rang out in the darkness.

"We lost Mark again!"

"That was George!"

"What? Scott's gone, too."

At this point, the driver had to swing his snow machine around in a U-turn, and the remaining soldiers in the hoods either hung on for dear life or were dislodged. Sometimes a driver called a truce and declared a search and rescue to find the missing in action.

As with the summer water battles, teams were somewhat fluid, depending on who arrived first to the rescue or had room in a particular hood. At times, I found myself in the opposing team's hood. Sometimes, we expended more effort attempting to stay in the hood than trying to unseat enemy troops. This was especially true if the drivers decided to leave the field and drive up and over the snow berm along a plowed driveway.

"Incoming!"

"Berm. Berm!"

"Hang on!"

Often this abrupt departure from a field discharged both hoods, at which point, an unofficial timeout was called, hoods righted, and we climbed back aboard.

Finally, we had had enough. As I trotted down the dark, snow-packed roadway into the circle of light in front of our house, I reviewed the evening's skirmish. Despite all this unsupervised mayhem, no body parts were lost, no long-lasting scars accumulated, or friendships permanently damaged. We would be back for more.

CHAPTER 4
FIRST GOAT HUNT

IN MANY WAYS, AUGUST OF 1965 marked my transition from a backyard plinker to a full-blown hunter. While I had already been on several hunts with Mom and Dad, I had always been an observer. As Dad drove down Swanson River or Funny River Road, I would sit in the back seat of the VW bus and look for moose.

Sometimes, Mom and Dad pulled me out of my elementary class to accompany them on early morning hunts. Hunting was not considered skipping school. Moose hunting was a community affair. Men, women, and even children talked about hunting successes or failures, where they had seen moose, and how the weather was affecting hunting. Moose was dinner for the homesteading families, as well as those who lived in town. A well-stocked freezer meant tasty roasts, steaks, meatloaf, and hamburgers throughout the year. And, it was our primary source of meat, except for occasional frozen chicken purchased from the store or Spam for breakfast. We didn't buy beef. Thus, when I returned to class later in the day, it was entirely normal for the teacher to ask if my parents had brought home meat for the table.

During those years, there were two moose seasons. The first season ran in September with the timeframe depending on the location of the hunt, while the second one was the last half of November. Hunting in September usually meant frosty mornings that warmed to above freezing by noon. Hunting in November was downright frigid. The VW's air-cooled engine provided little interior heat. When the temperature plummeted to minus 20 or 30 degrees, it became a deep freezer on wheels. We donned our heavy winter gear, which, without today's modern fabrics, was literally heavy.

Appearing quite tubby, I sat on the bench seat and gripped a plastic scraper with my doubly-mittened hand and scraped the frost from the window next to me. This opening temporarily granted me a view of the passing roadside. But, in short order, the little porthole frosted over. Again, I vigorously employed the scraper to regain my surveillance window. I was eager to be the hero who would call out "Moose"! Whenever I did so, Dad down-shifted and brought the mini-van to a halt to confirm the sighting was really a moose and not just another dark stump left by an uprooted tree.

Moose hunting was one thing. Mountain goat hunting was another. Moose were enormous animals, which meant packing out hundreds of pounds of meat. Hunters generally spotted these in flat lowlands or low hilly country. As their name implies, mountain goats, occupied the upper reaches of the mountains. They were cagey. They typically sought out the most inaccessible terrain where they were safe from predators. Another deterrent to hunting these animals was that the mountains generated their own unpredictable weather. Clouds, wind, and precipitation could come up suddenly. A hunter could carefully check a weather report before leaving home and dress appropriately, yet still get caught in an unpredicted downpour and risk hypothermia.

Evidently, Dad thought that at age nine, it was time for me to expand my hunting experience, and even though mountain goats were often challenging to hunt, he chose what he considered an *easy* goat hunt to do so. I already had experience with BB guns and a single-shot .22, and I knew basic gun safety. However, bigger game required more firepower. At some point, Dad had the stock of an 8mm Mauser shortened to accommodate my sister Naomi, whom he attempted to turn into his hunting buddy. She never warmed to the idea and to her relief, I was promoted to that position. The shortened stock put this high-powered rifle within my reach. After a few practice sessions behind the house on our 100-yard make-shift gun range, my ears rang, and my shoulder was sore. Nevertheless, he pronounced me ready to hunt.

The Kenai Mountains provide a home for two well-known alpine, big game species: the mountain goat and the Dall sheep, for which the hunting season opened on August 10. The mountain valleys hold numerous lakes, some fed by the runoff of melting glaciers, others strictly from snowmelt. Cooper Lake was one of these lakes and Dad selected it for our launch point.

Cooper Lake is six miles long, nestled in the heart of the Kenai Mountains, and accessible by road. It sits at 1,168 feet above sea level and is girdled on the northeastern edges with patches of evergreens consisting of hemlock and black spruce. Willows and alders border the rest of it. In this mountain setting, the lake is subject to strong winds that can make travel by watercraft hazardous. The road ends about two miles from the eastern end, where Dad wanted to start the ascent up the 4,900-foot mountain. There were only two options for getting to this starting point: either hike the shoreline, which was littered with driftwood and bordered with leg-tangling willows or take a small boat.

Dad had asked Jerry Near to come along on this hunt. I suspect it was for several reasons. First, Jerry had a square-stern canoe with a small outboard motor. In addition, another adult meant sharing the load when it came to packing out the meat from a successful hunt. It also meant having another rifle in the group in case we encountered a bear. Those last two items were tasks I could not do yet since I was pretty undersized and could not sling a real rifle over my shoulder without it dragging in the dirt behind me like a boat anchor. Jerry Near was Naomi's junior high school biology teacher. He was slightly taller and stockier than Dad's 5-foot-10 and 150-pound frame. Dad figured Jerry could carry his weight and half the goat's weight if it came down to it.

On the day of the hunt, we departed Soldotna before dawn with the canoe strapped to the top of the VW bus. We arrived at the lake one and a half hours later, just as the overcast sky started to brighten. It was a windless morning, and the lake reflected an inverted image of the mountain.

While I searched for flat rocks and skipped them on the lake, Dad and Jerry loaded the canoe with the minimal hunting gear needed for a one-day hunt: two packboards, rain ponchos, two rifles and ammunition, two sharp knives, a partial loaf of sliced white bread, a ring of bologna, matches, and a compass. I am not sure why we packed a compass. I never saw Dad use one, and not because we were never lost. It was just one of those things I figured every man had in his pack. In my little green army backpack, my hunting kit consisted of an extra pair of dry socks, a pocketknife, and a Hershey's chocolate bar.

The trip up the lake was uneventful, and we were soon winding our way uphill, following a game trail through the woods. I was excited! This was *my* hunt, my first big game hunt! It was also my first time in an Alaskan woodland other than on our homestead. One of the first things I noticed was the vegetation. The homestead had predominantly black spruce with a few stands of aspen. Here, under the canopy of spruce and hemlock evergreens, there were small ferns with delicate triangular-shaped leaves. The numerous black crowberry plants with spikey green stems made me feel like a giant viewing spruce trees from 1,000 feet up. There was a scattering of single-stemmed plants, about six inches high, with single berries that looked like tiny pumpkins.

The foliage and underbrush were not only novel to me, but the scents were unlike what I had experienced up to this point. For example, the hemlock had a more piney scent than the black spruce I was acquainted with. Alders had their own distinct perfume. They also had what appeared to be tiny pine cones. This environment was a whole new world, even better than Disney Land, which I had visited when we lived in California. Whenever the adults stopped to catch their breath, I examined these wonders in detail. Lagging at times, I poked around and occasionally added a specimen to my pack. Later, I would be so disappointed when I got home and found them withered and mangled.

Hunting habits kicked in, and Dad and Jerry talked quietly, even though there was no game to hear us. Dad shared past hunting experiences and outlined the details of our route as we wound our way upward.

"Mountain sheep and goats have sharp eyes. Goats will even post lookouts, so we don't want to be out in the open if we can help it. We will have to stay off the ridgeline going up. They like cliffs, too. They're not worth going after if they are in there."

After a few more steps, the monologue continued.

"It will be warm today, so the goats may be by snow up top. The bugs will be bad unless a breeze picks up."

The transition from trees and alders to alpine meadows and tundra was abrupt. Suddenly, I felt spongy moss beneath my feet and looked out to a limitless view. No longer hindered by the trees, a gentle wind carried the faint sounds of waterfalls in the alpine bowls above us. Looking back, I could see Cooper Lake below us. Since the trail had no signage or markers, Dad took special note of where we exited the treeline so we could find our way back down. Losing the trail would mean fighting through a tangle of alders, prickly, red-berried Devil's Club, and thick willows. Some hunters left a flag or cloth ribbon at the entrance to a trail, Dad just remembered, usually.

As we continued upward, we followed a broad-shouldered ridge, and the ground cover thinned. Large areas of creamy, brittle caribou moss (a type of lichen) covered the shale rocks. Here and there, patches of blueberry and crowberry bushes hugged the ground. Some plants had already started turning fall colors of orange, yellow, and maroon. It was as though Jack in the Beanstalk's giant had taken large cans of paint and tossed the contents across the mountainside.

By late morning, we were about 1,000 feet from the top of the mountain. Since we did not want to spook any wildlife, there had been no conversation for quite some time, even though we had not seen any wildlife. We guardedly skirted along the edge of the ridge to avoid presenting a silhouette. The climbing grew more difficult. We paused briefly to drink handfuls of water caught from a dripping patch of melting snow.

The terrain became nearly vertical. Maintaining a foothold on the steep mountainside kept my heart thumping. We traversed single-file across the shale. I looked downslope nervously. It was a long way down, and there was nothing to hold on to. At every step, the loose razorblade-like shale slid underfoot. I hesitated. Then froze. Dad proceeded without me. After about 50 feet, he glanced over his shoulder and noticed I was no longer riding his heels. He stopped. Without turning around, he backed up to where I was standing. "I'm afraid," I said almost inaudibly, mortified by my unexpected fear. Without a word, he held out his hand. Expelling my long-held breath, I gratefully reached up. Confidence replaced my alarm when I grabbed my father's hand. Thus reassured, I continued the upward trek.

Around noon, we reached the top of the mountain. The clouds had parted, and sunshine showered us with brightness and warmth.

From talking to other hunters, Dad knew that mountain goats usually ran uphill or toward the roughest terrain when threatened, and a hunter's strategy was to be at the highest point and hunt downward. With this in mind, we tentatively peered over the edges of the numerous ravines carved into the side of the mountain. As we made this methodical search, Dad suddenly motioned for us to crouch.

"They are on the snow," he whispered. As much as a mountain goat's coat appears pure white, it is actually slightly yellow when compared to the snow's whiteness.

Quietly, we removed our packs, dropped them gently to the ground, then slowly crept forward. Being short, I had to stand to peek between the shoulders of the crouched men. I could see several goats lying there. Goats are not very big, and lying down, they appear even smaller.

"They are about 150 yards away," said Dad, nearly inaudibly.

In addition to being nearby, they were also slightly downhill. It would be a relatively easy shot. Regardless, a hunter never wants the game to roll down the mountain after being shot and considers these factors before pulling the trigger.

He handed me the gun. The flat rocks made a good solid rest, which helped steady the rifle. As quietly as I could, I racked a shell into the chamber of the 8mm Mauser. I peered through the scope, zeroed in on the closest goat, and placed the crosshairs slightly behind the front shoulder. I vaguely remembered something about holding your breath. My heart pounded. I pulled the trigger. I do not recall hearing the shot or feeling the recoil. My full attention had been on hitting my mark.

The goats jumped up, looked around in bewilderment, then fled. All except the one I had targeted. It lay there unmoving. Dad and Jerry stood up. I laid the rifle aside, scrambled to my feet, and grinned up at Dad. He smiled at me broadly.

"Atta boy!"

I was elated!

"That was a very nice shot, young man," Jerry confirmed.

"Let's go see what he got." Dad was ready to move.

We retrieved our packs, walked over to the dead goat, and examined it. The shot had pierced the goat's heart, and it had made one leap before collapsing. Fortunately for us, it had not leaped over the cliff, a few feet away, where it would have fallen nearly 1,000 feet.

Dad made sure the goat was properly bled out, then said, "Let's eat! Where are the sandwiches?" Perhaps other people would have felt squeamish about eating after messing with blood and guts. Not a hunter. Not a doctor. Not a kid raised with hunting parents. We pulled out our bread and bologna, bowed our heads, and Dad thanked the Lord for a successful hunt and the lunch before us.

"Couldn't have asked for a better day," Jerry commented.

Dad wiped some crumbs from his lips with the sleeve of his flannel shirt and nodded.

"Those goats were right where we hoped to find them."

"Wait 'til l tell Mom!" I chimed in, hardly able to contain the excitement of the day.

Then, out came the knives and Dad proceeded to dress the animal, removing as much meat as possible. He dressed big game to produce the largest cuts of meat. Later, he and Mom could decide what could be cut into small roasts minute steaks, and so on. They would then grind the trimmings and odd bits and pieces into hamburger.

Our family did not hesitate to eat wild game, and unlike their domestic namesakes, these mountain goats have a very mild flavor, probably because mountain goats are not actually goats but are related to antelope.

As we headed back down the mountain, the sun was swinging westward and starting to dip. With two adults to pack out the meat, the hide, and the head, the hike down would be easy. Of course, I was still only packing my little knapsack, so maybe I remembered it a bit differently. Because we were no longer concerned about spooking game, our downward path was on the ridge rather than the steep side slopes. That meant walking with expanded views of the surrounding valleys and mountains in front of us. It also meant taking time to grab a handful of blueberries when we came across a patch.

Dad found the trail entrance into the woods just as he had remembered it, and we retraced our steps downward. With the sun setting and the tree branches overhead, it was much darker now. And, as the sun went down, so did the temperature. The damp chill penetrated my flannel shirt. I reached inside my pack for my jacket and slipped it over my head.

To me, the trail looked different than it had on the way up. The change in perspective surprised me, and at times, I wondered if we might be lost. Dad, however, did not seem concerned and carried on a casual conversation with Jerry. When we came out of the trees at the lake's edge, waves were lapping at the shoreline. An evening breeze had come up and blew unrestricted across the lake, stirring up the water. Waves two feet high were not a big deal to most small boats, but they could be disastrous in a canoe, especially if not approached properly.

"What do you think, Jerry?" Dad asked as he studied the waves in the dimming light.

"I think we'll be okay," Jerry replied. "I doubt that walking along the shoreline is really an option at this point."

"Well, let's load up and give it a shot," Dad decided.

Having flown with Dad in various types of inclement weather, I had unwavering faith in his ability to assess a situation and make the correct decision. If I had been a bit older, I might have asked him what he meant by "Give it a shot." It sounded suspiciously like, "Let's see if we tip over and get wet." Regardless, I sat on the bottom of the canoe, tucked between the packs. Dad stood at the bow and steadied the rocking craft. Jerry stepped into the stern and used a paddle to pivot it away from the shore. Dad kept the bow on the beach. Jerry started the motor and called to Dad to push off. Dad complied.

The trip back was not like it had been in the morning when the water was smooth, and we had motored along in the still water. It was as though we were on a completely different body of water. Jerry reduced the speed to keep the canoe's bow from kicking up spray, although we were getting splashed anyway. He guided the canoe along the shoreline, attempting to stay in shallow water in case we capsized. To reach our parked vehicle, however, meant crossing a small bay and there would be no one around to rescue us if we capsized in the ice-cold water. None of us spoke. It was so dark. How could Dad and Jerry see where to go? Where was the shoreline? Where was the VW bus? Jerry throttled back so he could speak above the engine noise. Through the slapping of the waves and hissing wind, he hollered to Dad, "Do you see it?"

"Not yet," Dad shouted. Jerry throttled up slightly. Almost immediately we spotted the dim shape of the VW a short way up the beach.

"It's there! It's over there! I exclaimed. We were going to make it.

Turning toward the beach, Jerry adeptly brought our rocking canoe to shore. The men transferred the gear to the micro-bus, lifted the canoe on top, and strapped it in place. Meanwhile, I rummaged about the contents of the VW for a blanket to wrap around my damp shoulders. When I'd shot the goat, I had felt like a real hunter, even a bit like a man. But now, I was a tired little boy.

As we wound our way down from Cooper Lake, the drone of the VW's motor and the meager but welcome warmth from the heater, conspired with fatigue, and I was soon happily asleep. I'd done it. My first goat hunt was complete. And I'd made my father proud.

CHAPTER 5

ADVENTURES AT SILVER SALMON CREEK

THE SUMMER I WAS 10, Dad and flew across Cook Inlet to Silver Salmon Creek and stopped by Wayne and Sandy Bells' to fish for silver salmon. Sandy's parents, Ken and Margaret Kruger, worked the site with them. Our families helped establish the Soldotna Bible Chapel, so our paths crossed often. In addition, when not on the fish site, Sandy worked in Dad's office as the receptionist. The Bells had three sons: Mark, my age; David three years younger; and Greg, three years younger still.

Greg Bell, Mark Bell, Mark Gaede, and David Bell with Two King Salmon
(Picture courtesy of the Wayne and Sandy Bell family)

Their fish site was a flight of 65 miles across Cook Inlet from our homestead. The beaches around Silver Salmon were generously wide, lengthy, and mostly billiard-table smooth. Dad landed his blue-and-white, four-place M4 Maule Rocket near the Bell's two cabins. The Maule, which Dad had purchased after selling the Piper PA-14, was not like Dad's previous airplanes. This one had a six-cylinder engine that rumbled and roared. It had four seats, so I got to sit up front with Dad. And it was fast—150 mph fast. Not the plodding 80 mph of a J-3. No, sir. This thing moved. Spacious, too. We could stuff all kinds of things inside—more than essential emergency gear. It had plenty of room for fishing rods, sleeping bags, and any treasure we might spot as we winged our way up and down the coast: treasures such as driftwood, lengths of thick rope, and orange plastic buoys or aqua glass balls used as floats for fish nets. The Maule was a real airplane! I was plenty proud my dad owned it.

We disembarked while Wayne and his boys walked over to greet us. Dad pulled out two fishing rods rigged for the hard-hitting silvers, and I grabbed the familiar dull-green metal tackle box. We all scuffed through the loose mix of sand and gravel on our way to the mouth of the creek. Dad and Wayne exchanged pleasantries.

"How's fishing been?" Dad wanted to know.

"Well, it's been slow, but I expect it to pick up next week when the tides are better," Wayne told him. Wayne was about my dad's height but of thicker build. He wore dark green, knee-high rubber boots that partially covered his denim blue jeans. A heavy vest topped his plaid flannel shirt, and a blue hat covered his thinning hair.

His comment made me wonder if he was fishing on the wrong side of the boat. Maybe he needed to cast his net on the other side like Jesus had instructed his disciples. At that point, I didn't realize the Bell's nets never left the beach.

I pushed aside their conversation, which moved on to the price of salmon.

Dad set on getting a line in the water, I hurried to the creek. I set the tackle box down, popped open the lid, and selected a large red-and-white fish seducer with a huge treble hook dangling from it. I may have been only nine, but I knew my way around a tackle box. All those hours down at Slikok Creek paid off. With familiar ease, I snapped the lure to the swivel tied to the end of the 15-pound monofilament line. Then, I stood at the creek's edge, made my backcast, swung the rod forward, and watched the lure sail out over the water. The Bell boys wandered around me, chattering about this and that. After the lure plunked into the water, I began my retrieval, anticipating the heavy tug of a 10-pound silver attacking my irresistible lure.

"Come on. Bite!" I encouraged the fish, hoping no one heard me.

After fishing unsuccessfully for some time, I prepared to cast yet again. I swung the rod over my shoulder, then whipped it forward. I watched for the flash of red and white and listened for the muted hiss of the line leaving the reel. No flash. No hiss. Something was wrong. I looked up at the tip of my rod. The line at the end was taut, behind me, not forward where I expected it to be. That sure wasn't right. I turned to follow the line. The huge treble hook on the red-and-white lure hung from Mark's cheek. I had failed to check behind me before I started my backcast and had smitten my buddy. I stared at him, mortified. Mark didn't cry or exclaim in pain.

"Mark...I'm so sorry...," I said.

He stood mute, staring at me, perhaps in shock.

Apparently, the adults had witnessed this unintended catch. They immediately stopped talking, and Dad rushed over to evaluate the patient.

"I am going to take him back to town to extract the hook," Dad told Mark's dad.

Feeling mighty embarrassed, I gathered up my fishing gear, carried it to the plane, and slunk into the backseat. Mark rode up front with Dad. I spent the flight back remorseful and repentant.

I'm not sure what transpired between my parents and the Bells after that. Maybe Mom and Dad paid blood money, or perhaps they promised to withhold my fishing privileges until I was old, like age 13.

My "backyard" was an 80-acre homestead. The Bells' "backyard" was a set-net fish site on Silver Salmon Creek. In contrast to our homestead, it was on the ocean with the scent of salty seaweed, miles of sandy beaches, driftwood, and bears, all set against a backdrop of the ragged Aleutian Range. Regardless of hooking Mark Bell in the face, the following summer found me back at Silver Salmon Creek. This time it would be for two glorious weeks. Dad approached the Bells, and they agreed to host me for two weeks. Little did I know I would be indebted to this family for giving me the time of my life, with memories forever. It was here I learned the rhythm of the tides; predictable, yet ever-changing. It was here I learned to love the scent of salty air and the sound of rushing waves. It was here I learned that grizzlies owned the land, and we were tolerated visitors.

There are two methods of commercial salmon fishing in Cook Inlet: drifting and set-netting. Drift fishing involves a boat used to pick fish from a net that drifts with the tide. It is not anchored. Set-net fishing utilizes a fixed (set) net with one end anchored offshore and the other up on the beach. Fish swimming along the shore encounter the set-net and become entangled.

Silver Salmon Creek lies at the foot of Mount Iliamna (Ill-ee-AHM-nuh), an 11,000-foot active volcano in the Aleutian (Uh-LOO-shun) Range on the west side of Cook Inlet. The creek's name, while unimaginative, is aptly chosen; it is a creek where silver salmon, or coho, spawn. West-side set-netters dot the shoreline for some 70 miles, beginning south of Drift River to the north and ending at Chinitna (Chin-IT-nah) Bay to the south.

Silver Salmon Creek, nearly in the middle, was the location of three fish sites, with Wayne and Sandy's site right at the mouth of the creek.

Dad flew me over one evening after work. Beforehand, he had checked the weather, and, just as importantly, the tides. There was no need to make the 45-minute jaunt if a high tide covered the beach and we couldn't land. Mom helped me pack. Her list included an extra pair of pants, an extra shirt, three pairs of mismatched socks (she was looking for ones without holes), a light sweater, my toothbrush, and a seldom-used comb. My contribution included a jacket, black knee-high rubber boots, and tennis shoes. Mom also handed Dad a paper grocery sack with a head of lettuce, some tomatoes, and a plastic bag of homemade cinnamon rolls. Isolated fish sites like the Bells' were supplied only by air, and fresh produce was a luxury. But, for me, the most essential items for this stay were in the small brown paper bag I clutched in my hand.

For many people I knew, life revolved around airplanes. Therefore, it was only natural we kids were attracted to them, too. I spent hours playing with simple balsa wood airplanes. These had the same basic components as the bush planes I was acquainted with, but more rudimentary: a skinny stick for a fuselage, spindly wire landing gear, wings, tail feathers, rudder, propeller, and a rubber band motor. Granted, real bush planes were a bit more complicated, but not by much. I knew the Bell boys would be excited to have these imitation airplanes to play with, so I bought some to take along. There were several different models to choose from, and I used my years of experience to make age-appropriate selections. Mark and I were the oldest, so I decided on two top-of-the-line Sleek Streak kits for 25 cents apiece. For David, I purchased a Skeeter for 15 cents. It was a wee bit smaller, although still rubber band powered, but had no landing gear. I bought a simple glider for Greg with the dime I had saved on the Skeeter. I gripped these valuables ever so tightly.

Thus provisioned, Dad and I climbed aboard the Maule Rocket and blasted off.

We touched down and taxied to a halt in front of the Bells' cabins. The boys scrambled through the soft sand to see who had arrived. I toted my bag of clothes and cautiously guarded the paper bag that held the fragile airplanes. Dad carried the grocery sack. As we approached the cabin, Mark's mom opened the door.

"Come in, come in!" she beckoned vigorously.

"Hello, Sandy," Dad greeted her.

Sandy Bell Making Cranberry Jam
(Picture courtesy of the Wayne and Sandy Bell family)

He handed the diminutive redhead the sack Mom had prepared. She peeked inside, and her face lit up in delight.

"Oh, Doctor Gaede. You shouldn't have!"

Dad smiled. "Ruby says hello."

She turned to me. "Hello, Mark. Why don't you set your things over there." She motioned to a spot at the back of the cabin.

I followed her instructions.

"Mark," I heard her say. I turned to her... then realized she was addressing *her* Mark, not me. "Why don't you take Mark outside and show him around."

With two Marks around, this could be confusing.

Wayne and Sandy Bell's Cabin at Silver Salmon Creek

(Picture courtesy of Wayne and Sandy Bell family)

I stepped out the door for my orientation. Before following Mark farther, I looked back toward the beach where Dad had parked the Maule. I could only see the tip of the propeller. Tides had piled the beach sand up in a low barrier along this stretch of shoreline. Clumps of tall sawgrass stems topped with wheat-like seeds nodded in the breeze. A tangled covering of wild sweet peas sprawled everywhere across the shifting sand. The violet-purple flowers, prominent earlier in summer, had been replaced by pods swelling with peas. Here and there, tree trunks lay, stripped of bark and limb. Smooth and gray, they were half-buried in the sand. The cabins sat behind this sandy barrier, which offered a measure of shelter from the ever-present wind. The soft bank also muted the sound of the waves crashing at high tide when the water was closest to the cabins. I'd soon learn that the set-netter's everyday life consisted of daily wind, saltwater, and sand.

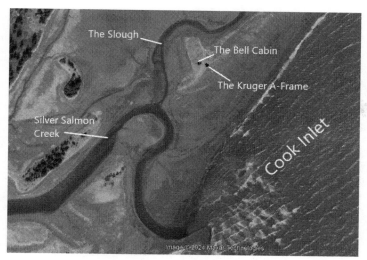

Map of the Bell's Fish Site

"You coming?" Mark called. His brother, David, tagged behind him.

Mark led us away from the beach and down a hard-beaten path past two weathered structures with doors and flat-slanted roofs. One was slightly taller than the other.

"This is the outhouse," he announced, pointing at the shorter of the two structures.

I had guessed as much already, although I did not know why they needed two unless one was for girls and one for boys.

"Why do you have two?"

David looked at Mark and snickered. Mark laughed. "No, no, no. That's the smokehouse."

"Oh," I said. I had heard the term before, but since we didn't have one on the homestead, I was not entirely sure what it meant. I had seen people smoke cigarettes and had listened to my parents' disapproval. Did Mark's dad smoke cigarettes in there?

"Don't "go" in there," David advised. He and Mark exchanged meaningful glances and then giggled.

Mark, David, and Greg Bell by the Silver Salmon Creek Smokehouse
(Picture courtesy of the Wayne and Sandy Bell family)

The moment passed and Mark continued to follow the trail bracketed with low grass and more scattered driftwood. There were no alders or trees to block my view, just shallow pockets here and there collecting blown sand and marooned flotsam. About 100 feet farther ahead was another shoreline. This slough filled with brackish water at high tide. The water's edge had a variety of plants, all unknown to me, and they immediately captured my attention. I reached down and plucked a thick, narrow leaf from a small plant at my feet.

"What's this?" I asked Mark.

"That's goose tongue," he replied.

I surveyed the crop of goose tongue at my feet. It evoked a picture of tongueless geese. I laughed.

Mark's brow wrinkled. "What's so funny?"

"Where are all the geese?" I asked, holding up the blade in my hand.

Now, we all laughed. Mark continued his tour, and I became so absorbed I did not notice Dad take off and disappear to the north.

After a simple but tasty dinner, Mark's dad gave us instructions. His boys already knew these things, so it was for my benefit. "You boys can go outside and play for another hour. When you hear us call, come straight back to the cabin."

Then he spoke to me directly. "Before you come in, use the outhouse. When you kids are back in, don't leave until the morning. If you need to use the outhouse at night, there is a honey bucket under the bed."

I nodded.

He then turned and headed back outdoors.

I knew about a honey bucket. We had one in the homestead house before the plumbing was completed. Since the cabin had no interior walls, only a curtain partition that separated the two sleeping areas from the kitchen and dining area, I could not imagine using the bucket in the middle of the night and in a common room.

Mark and I followed him outside. We shuffled to the top of the barrier of sand, plopped down on a log, and looked out to sea. The seabed was shallow and flat here. When the tide went out, as it was now, the waterline lay 300 yards or more away. Rather than the pounding of waves, I heard the sound of rushing water in the distance, like a mountain stream, but with more ebb and flow. I knew that sometime during the night, the tide would turn, and the salty water would climb back up the beach.

The breeze had laid down as the sun sank, and a few white-sock flies circled our heads. I batted them away.

"Why can't we use the outhouse at night?" I asked Mark.

Without hesitation, Mark stated seriously, "Bears."

"Oh," was all I said. I knew about bears. Dad had three bear skin rugs nailed to the wall back home. I had watched the home movies of him hunting the massive white polar bear and the shaggy-furred, long-clawed spring grizzly.

Mark provided more detail.

"These are grizzlies. They come out at night and walk the beach. Sometimes right next to the cabin." He paused to watch my reaction. Sometimes, you can hear them claw on the cabin. Did you see the boards with nails sticking out around the windows?"

I absorbed this information, but if Mark's father was not overly concerned, neither would I be. Though, I knew if nature called at night, I would use the honey bucket.

Too quickly, the hour passed, and we heard Mark's mom call us in. Mark and I hurried to the outhouse, tended what became an evening ritual, and ran laughing for the cabin door.

My sleeping bag felt cozy when I wriggled into it. I found the pillow Mark's mom had pulled out for me to use, slid it under my head, and turned toward Mark, who was in the lower bunk in the boys'"bedroom."

"What are we going to do tomorrow?" I whispered.

"I don't know. Maybe wade in the slough," he whispered back.

"Are there fish in there?" I wanted to know.

"Oh, some sticklebacks, bull beads, maybe a flounder." Mark knew his slough. His mom interrupted our planning session.

"Okay, boys. Go to sleep."

The morning and the evening were the first day. And it was good.

Mark's dad was already gone by the time we woke up. Our speedy breakfast may have lacked proper etiquette, but we were efficient and ready to go. I slid into my knee-high rubber boots, and the other two older boys did the same. Greg saw the bigger boys headed out the door and wanted to go along.

"Mom, make Greg stay here," Mark begged.

"Greg let's go see what Grandma is doing," Mark's mom suggested.

With Greg's attention successfully diverted, the three of us trotted down to the tidal slough, our boots flip-flopping as we hurried.

At the slough's edge, Mark stepped confidently into the water and waded out to where it reached halfway up his boots. I followed, watching the puffs of muddy water that billowed with each step. The bottom felt firmer underfoot than the mucky bottom of the gravel pits back home.

"Stickleback!" Mark yelled.

A small shadow darted this way and that under the water's surface. We waded a little farther.

"I see one. Over there. Wait, there's two!" I shouted enthusiastically.

David felt left out. "I wanna' see," he demanded.

"Stay back," Mark cautioned. "You'll scare the fish."

"I will not," David protested and headed in our direction.

We waded and chased fish until Mark made an observation. "Tide's coming in."

We sloshed back toward the shore. Our fish-hunting expedition had led us several hundred feet up the slough, and it took me a moment to get my bearings. We ambled back toward our entry point, and I noticed some goose tongue plants were submerged. I watched the water's edge closely as it inched slowly up the bank. It reminded me of our bathtub filling with water on Saturday nights. This slough, however, was a huge bathtub!

Back on the trail to the cabins, Mark had another idea. "You wanna see some bear tracks?"

"Sure," I replied. We didn't have bear tracks on the homestead. But this was not my backyard; it was a seaside backyard.

"Everybody knows what bear tracks look like," grumbled David.

"Follow me," said Mark. Off he ran with me close behind.

David may not have been excited about bear tracks, but he joined us, nonetheless.

We headed back down the slough toward the mouth of Silver Salmon Creek.

Mark stopped and pointed to an indentation at his feet. "Here's some."

I stepped closer. There was more than one, and the tracks were large enough for me to step inside of…with both feet. Impressive!

"Those are pretty big."

Mark nodded.

The soft, dry sand above the high tide line left ill-defined tracks. Where a pawprint was closer to the water and in the moist sand, I could see the outline of the toes. Beyond the toes were claw marks. These prints were intimidating but also so fascinating! I studied the far bank, which rose about 50 feet across the swiftly moving creek. There were prints over there, too; prints that led up the bank and left a shadowy trail in the tall grass before the dark, dense line of alders swallowed them up. Is that where the bears lived, I wondered?

We continued to traipse along the edge of the creek, picking up sticks, tossing them as far as we could into the water, and watching them bob as the current carried them out of sight around a bend. Seagulls cried overhead, and the sun shone brightly. What better day could young boys want?

"Hey!" Mark exclaimed suddenly. "I'm hungry. Let's go back to the cabin."

We were kids. We didn't have watches. We did not know how to tell time from the sun's position. Besides, it never stayed in the same position from one week to the next. Our internal clocks served our primary purposes. Mark's alarm had just gone off and announced it was time to eat.

We trotted cross-country, hopping over driftwood and swishing through prolific sweet peas until we stumbled onto the beaten path back to the cabins.

Sprinting past Mark and me, David reached the cabin first, leaned against the doorframe, and between gasps, declared victory.

"I won! I won!"

"I let you," countered Mark.

Before the war of words could intensify, their mom swung the door open and intervened.

"Boys, BOYS! Take your muddy boots off before coming in. Wash your hands, too."

"Okay, Mom," David and Mark replied in unison.

A metal washbasin, half-full of clean water from the hand-dug well and pitcher pump, rested on a waist-high wooden stand that leaned against the front of the cabin. A well-used bar of soap lay beside the basin, and a hand towel hung from a nail nearby.

We did as we were told, before going inside to check out the menu. The bottom of the basin gave evidence of our fun morning with slough mud and salty sand.

After lunch, I remembered the balsa airplanes stowed in the paper bag.

"Hey, guys. I brought some airplanes. You want to play with them?" I asked.

I received an expected and eager response. Even little Greg joined in. I liked Greg. Of the three brothers, he was the only one shorter than me. Cute and cheerful, too.

Retrieving the paper bag, I handed out the kits. Mark and David tore the ends off the plastic packaging, gently punched the die-cut pieces from the balsa wood sheets and began assembling the aircraft. To all of us boys, these were *not* toys. They were real airplanes. They had wings and they flew. I saw Greg needed help. I put together his glider and handed it back to him. Turning my attention to my kit, I quickly constructed my own airplane.

"I can't find my wheels," said David. "Why doesn't mine have wheels?"

I had not counted on him noticing so quickly.

"Your kit didn't have any," I said evenly.

He would not let it go. "Why not?"

I was not about to tell him I had not thought it would matter to him, so I tried a different tack. "Yours is faster that way. Our wheels will slow ours down."

This fact was true, and every Alaskan boy who had been around airplanes knew it. Airplanes with retractable gear were much faster than airplanes with landing gear that was always down.

David may have been a few years younger, but he was sharp. "So, how do I land?"

I gave up and turned my attention to Mark, who had selected a tiny patch of beach for our runway. We had wandered oceanward to the side that faced Cook Inlet. The mushy sand was generally smooth; however, these aeronautical wonders had wing spans of only 16 inches and a chip of wood, a pebble, or a blade of sawgrass would spell disaster. Of course, with a faint breeze, we only needed a three-foot runway. Mark wound his rubber band motor until he had a full row of knots, rubber band knots, not knots as in a measurement of speed. Then, holding the stick fuselage in one hand and the propeller in the other, he set the airplane down on the runway, facing into the wind, of course. He released the airplane and propeller. The mini bush plane leaped ahead and climbed steeply to the right until the rubber band unwound, after which it glided more or less straight ahead, dipping and weaving as the breeze came and went. Eventually, it got close to the ground. We held our breath. Would it stay upright when it touched down? Or flip over on its back?

On the rare occasion one of our airplanes landed successfully, it called for a huge celebration.

"Wow! Did you see that?" we would shout excitedly as we ran up to inspect the tracks the wheels left in the sand.

Yes, takeoff was easy. Landing upright was often pure luck, something early aviators might have identified with.

The takeoff and landing contest continued for several days until cumulative damage from flying into logs, repetitive flip-overs, or mishandling, rendered an airplane no longer airworthy. Then, it was time to scavenge parts from other airplanes. Greg's became spare parts when he accidentally stepped on it. He was in tears and saw this as a loss of playing with the big boys. On the other hand, I recognized that tail feathers had just become available. These refabrications continued until there were not enough parts to launch even one airplane into the air.

Too quickly, the sun disappeared behind Mount Iliamna, and we were back behind the locked cabin door.

The morning and the evening were the second day. And it was really good.

"I'd like you boys to come help Grandpa and me pick fish," Wayne said after lunch on the third day.

I did not know what "picking fish" meant, but everything so far had been a lot of fun. The three of us older boys climbed into the back of a weathered, rusted old stubby-bed Jeep that had been barged over at one time. Mark's grandpa waited by the front passenger door. His slight frame was covered almost entirely by dark rubberized bibs, although I could see a red wool jacket peeping behind the bib's suspenders. He did not wear a hat, and I thought his head must always be cold since the only hair he had was closely cropped above his ears and along the back part of his head. A day's worth of salt-and-pepper facial scruff gave him a rugged appearance. Satisfied that we were safely in the back, he pulled himself onto the passenger seat. Wayne swung into the driver's seat and told us to hang on. He fired up the old Jeep, ground it into gear, and pulled away from the cabins.

Up we spun over the sandy barrier, following a vehicle track onto the beach proper, where Wayne turned to the north. About a quarter-mile later, he braked the Jeep to a stop, stepped out, and slammed the door shut. Grandpa slid out the other side. The two crunched through the gravel to a long, large net that lay stretched out on the beach. We boys jumped out and followed. Above the high tide line was a post with a rope that ran from it to where the net began. The net continued over 150 feet toward the ocean. At this moment, the tide was out, and the net lay fully exposed. Caught in the net were a variety of 30 to 40 fish, the largest being nearly my size. I pondered this for a moment or two. I had to catch my fish one at a time. Somehow, using a big net seemed like cheating.

"What do you do with all the fish?" I asked Mark, watching his dad and grandpa pull fish from the net, some rapidly, some requiring more work.

"Dad sells them," Mark replied.

"Who buys them?" I asked.

"Some guy in a boat comes along. Then Dad and Grandpa pew them into his boat."

"What do you mean, pew?" That sounded rather disgusting.

"They have a pole with a point on it. They stick the fish in the head and toss them into the other boat."

"Oh, like a pitchfork?"

"What's a pitchfork?"

I described one of the pitchforks we used to put up hay on the homestead.

"Yeah, like that, but it only has one fork."

That drew a picture in my head.

"Get over here and help pick these fish." Mark's dad would not tolerate any slackers, not that he had said this in a mean way.

Mark, David, and I joined the two adults.

Mark showed me how to work the net up and over the slippery gills and head and toss the fish in the gravel behind us. Most of the fish were already dead, though a few still jerked and twitched. I approached another stranded fish.

"That's a silver," Mark told me.

"I thought they were all silvers. This is Silver Salmon Creek, right?" Mark laughed.

"We catch all different kinds of salmon. It just depends. Here, let me show you. See the silver streaks on the tail? That tells you it's a silver."

Well, that made sense, unlike a pew stick.

I freed another silver before coming to a fish that had worked its way about halfway through the net. I could not get the net to move forward or backward. Wayne came over to assist.

"That's a sea-run Dolly Varden," he said, leaning over. "It's smaller than the salmon and gets farther into the mesh. See how blue it looks compared to the salmon?"

He held in his hand a short wooden handle with a curved hook on it and used that to work the net back over the head of the fish, which he freed and tossed away from the other fish.

"Why did he throw that fish away?" I quietly asked Mark.

"Nobody will buy it."

I wondered why but didn't say anything. It was a pretty big fish. I would not have thrown it back if I had caught it.

After we picked the fish out of the net and slowly started back to the Jeep, I spied another abandoned fish and went to check it out. Oh! A small shark!

"Mark, come here!" I called exuberantly.

He ran over to where the shark was parked.

"It's a shark!" I told him.

"Oh, that's a dogfish."

I had spent enough time in the World Book Encyclopedia to know what a shark looked like. I had never seen a real one, but this thing had gill slits, a mouth back under its nose, triangular dorsal fins, and a swept tail. It looked like a shark to me.

"Pretty sure it's a shark," I insisted.

"That is a dogfish!" said Mark emphatically.

I reached down and brushed the creature with my finger. The skin felt like sandpaper. "That's a shark!"

"Dad!" Mark called for backup.

Mark's dad changed course and joined us. Mark presented his case. "Mark says that's a shark. It's a dogfish, right?"

Mark's dad smiled and pronounced his verdict. "You are both right. It's a shark that is called the spiny dogfish."

The morning and the evening were the third day, and it was very, very good.

Our forays in and along the slough took an attention-grabbing turn one day. During our wading excursions, we sometimes flushed out small, flat flounders, perhaps six to seven inches across. The drab olive-colored skin on their upper sides matched the bottom of the slough. When they held still, it was difficult to spot them.

"We need spears," Mark said. "Then we could catch one."

That sounded like a terrific idea.

"What will we use?"

"Follow me to the tool shed," he replied.

Near the outhouse and smokehouse, was a tool shed. Mark opened the door, walked inside, and started searching the shelves. I stood in the doorway. In the dim light, I could see benches along the walls with lots of boxes on and under them and coils of rope, too. It looked a lot like the workbenches in my dad's hangar.

"We need some big sticks for the handles. Go find some, and I'll get other things," he instructed me.

I went on a stick hunt and discovered that all the desired-sized sticks had disappeared. Maybe we had thrown them all in the water by now. The remaining ones were too big or too small. Finally, I settled on two I thought were close enough in dimension and ran back to the shed. Mark stood waiting with a hammer and nails.

"Here. Set the end on this rock, and I'll pound a nail into it," Mark directed.

I selected one stick and steadied it as Mark took a two-inch nail, held it against the end of the stick, and tapped it with the hammer. After a slip-up or two, he hammered it in until only an inch remained. Then he smashed the nail head flat and created a barbed spear tip of sorts. Satisfied with the results, we prepared the second spear. Now armed with what we hoped were lethal weapons, we hurried back to the slough, only to find the tide had covered our hunting grounds. We would have to try later.

The opportunity arrived the very next day. Mark and I waded out, our eyes in constant motion, searching for movement on the bottom. After chasing a pair of smaller flounders, I spotted another one.

"It's a big one!" I shouted and motioned with my spear.

It was huge. Maybe 12-inches-across-huge. To two boys armed with stick-and-nail weaponry, it was a monster.

"Do you see it?" I prompted him.

"Don't lose it!" He shouted.

"There it is. Don't scare it."

We froze.

Now, with a fix on the Leviathan's hiding spot, we closed in on its position. As stealthy as four legs in the water can be, we crept near our prey. I drew back my stick and plunged it into the fish.

"I got it, Mark. I got it! What do I do?" I was frantic. I didn't want to lose the thrashing flounder I had pinned to the bottom. I thought if I raised the spear, the fish would fall off. If I tried to hold it against the bottom and slide it toward the bank, it might also swim free.

"Just toss it like you are pewing fish."

I held the fish in place with my spear, sidled around it until I faced the shore, gritted my teeth, and flipped the tip of the stick up. The furiously flopping flounder flew through the air and landed on the bank with a satisfying smack. Mark and I raced ashore to subdue it before it could thrash its way back into the water. Boy, were we proud.

"We need to cook it," I said. After all, that was the way hunting and fishing worked.

"I'll go ask Mom."

He hurried back to consult with the master chef.

I knew my mom always had other things to eat, not just a piece of fish or a chunk of moose. What could I add? Not Jello. Not bread. What about peas? I had snacked on wild, raw ones the day before, and they tasted like the frozen peas I had eaten at David Isaak's house once.

The master chef sent Mark back with an ample piece of tinfoil and instructions that sounded a lot like "Don't bring that fish back here." Mark pulled out his pocketknife, sawed off the fish's head, pulled out the few guts it had, and tossed them into the slough. He rinsed off the dressed fish before positioning it on the tinfoil. I curled the edges of the foil toward the fish to keep it from sliding onto the sand.

"We need a fire. Can we make one here?" I asked.

"Sure. I brought matches."

We built a small teepee with short sticks and filled the inside with bits of dry grass.

Mark dug a matchstick out of his pocket, struck it across a stone, and applied the burning sliver to the grass. The teepee burst into flames. We added larger sticks to build a bed of coals.

"I'm going to pick some peas," I informed Mark.

"Oh, good idea. It will take a lot of pods though. Those peas are pretty small."

Mark tended the fire while I wandered off to collect sweet pea pods, which sprawled nearly everywhere. I searched the vines and chose fatter pods with plumper peas inside them. By the time the coals burned down for baking, I had picked a half-cup of peas. I added those to the slab of flounder and wrapped more foil over the top. Together, Mark and I gingerly placed our fish on the coals. Then we sat on our haunches and waited.

After what seemed like hours to us, Mark asked, "Is it done yet?"

"I don't know."

"How will we know?"

"I don't know." I pulled back the foil with a stick and poked at our meal. "I don't think it's ready."

Somehow, I'd attained the role of Grill Master, and now Mark believed whatever I said.

Eventually, a tantalizing aroma wafted out of the foil.

"It *has* to be done now!" I said, feeling my stomach rumble.

Carefully, I peeled back the foil and again poked the fish. The skin parted, exposing white, flakey meat.

"Help me move it off the fire, Mark."

Together, we slid the foil off the coals. Eagerly, we stripped back the skin, pinched off pieces of the tender flesh, and popped the morsels into our mouths. We turned to each other with slow grins. It was some of the best fish I had ever eaten—and we had just proven we could provide a meal for ourselves.

Sloshing around in the slough, throwing sticks in the creek, and watching for bears became a familiar routine. Sometimes, though, the slough was too deep, or we grew tired of tossing sticks. In moments like those, boredom threatened our day, and we got creative. It usually started with "Have you ever...?"

"Have you ever put a match in an empty .22 shell and made it 'bang'?" Mark asked me.

"Huh, uh," I replied.

I had heard .22 cartridges go "bang," but never an empty one.

"Follow me. I'll show you something."

Mark darted inside the tool shed and reemerged with the hammer. Locating a convenient flat stone outside the shed entrance, he knelt down, laid the hammer on the ground, and dug around in his pockets. He produced a .22 casing. It glinted in the sun as he rested it on the stone. He rummaged some more in his pockets. I squatted across from him, picked up the casing, and examined it. Yep. It was empty: open at one end and closed at the other. The closed end had a little dimple along the rim. It looked safe to me, and I set it back down. Mark held up a wooden match. What else did he keep in those pockets? He was like a walking hardware store.

"Okay. Watch this," he told me.

He picked up the empty casing, inserted the matchhead, and snapped the matchstick flush with the open edge of the casing. I leaned forward to examine his craftsmanship, then rocked back on my heels to give him more space. Placing the assembly back on the stone, he hammered the open end flat, crimping the matchhead in place.

"Here goes!" he warned. "Stand back!"

He stepped away until the stone was at arm's length. I observed his caution and scooted backward a bit more. He swung the hammer. It missed the casing and hit the stone. The casing spun off into the sand. Mark located it, placed the casing back on the stone, and raised the hammer again. Down it came. POP! Ha! It was much louder than a cap gun "pop," although not as sharp as an actual .22 being fired. What fun!

"Do you have any more?" I asked.

He nodded. "Here, you try it."

Mark handed me another empty casing and a match. I repeated the procedure and laid the casing on the stone.

"Get ready!" I issued my own warning.

I swung…and missed. The casing rolled off the stone. I tried again and missed. I needed to get closer. I repositioned myself and swung one more time. This time, the hammer struck the casing and with a rewarding loud "POP." But…something hit the left side of my face, between the lower part of my cheek and my nose. By reflex, my hand reached up to touch the spot. It came away red.

"Nice one! Let's make another.…"

Mark stopped mid-sentence. His smile vanished when he saw the trickle of blood on my cheek. I held the sleeve of my shirt against my wound, and we looked for clues to explain what had happened. We found the smashed casing. It was missing the flat end. It must have blown off when the matchhead ignited.

That put an end to the exciting, though brief, adventure. Fortunately, before long, my wound ceased bleeding. We slunk over to the cabin to use the wash basin. I scrubbed my cheek and bloody shirtsleeve to remove the evidence. With the drama behind us, we headed down the familiar path to the slough. Traveling side-by-side, Mark turned to me.

"Have you ever…?"

I knew Dad was not going to pick me up for several days yet, so I was surprised when Wayne found us out exploring and asked me to come back to the cabin.

"You need to pack up your things," he stated with no additional information.

Maybe he had heard about the .22 incident, and I was being banished. But on arrival at the cabin, a man I did not recognize was standing outside the open doorway. I hurried inside and stuffed my few belongings in the bag I had arrived with. When I finished rolling and tying off my sleeping bag, Wayne came over and gave me the unexpected news.

"Mark, your father was in an airplane accident. This man will fly you back home."

I stared at him, mute and numb, then stumbled out of the cabin and followed the pilot to the beach where his plane was parked. I do not recall flying along the coast or climbing to cross Cook Inlet, though I know we did. I could not believe it. What had happened to my dad? He could not crash! He never got hurt. My mind was still racing in circles when the pilot landed on the homestead strip and taxied to the house where Mom had walked out to meet us. She was not smiling. I unlatched my seatbelt buckle, scrambled out of the airplane, and ran toward her.

"Mom! What happened to Daddy!"

My father would recover, but the blue-and-white Maule Rocket would never again be a part of his adventures. Regardless, the memories I made at Silver Salmon Creek would never be lost, and decades later, I would revisit those moments of sea breeze ruffling my hair, seagulls screaming overhead, and the smell of fish when picking nets.

The Crashed Maule Rocket

CHEECHAKO NEWS

August 4, 1967

Forced Landing Injures
Soldotna Doctor, Druggist

A Soldotna doctor was the pilot in four-place Maule Rocket, which crash landed Wednesday morning about four miles off the Sterling Highway out of Soldotna, injuring two of the three persons aboard.

Dr. Elmer Gaede, pilot, and Lee bowman, local pharmacist, both received multiple lacerations of the head and face and nearly identical injuries to the spine.

Dave Parks, who came to Alaska about a month ago from Michigan, was seated in the back seat and was uninjured.

Dr. Gaede was returning from Seward where he and Dr. Paul, his associate in the clinic at Soldotna, had been engaged in surgery at the Seward Hospital.

Engine failure is believed to have been the cause of the forced landing which occurred at about10:30 a.m. between the homes of Dr. Calvin Fair and "Chuck" Foster on Forest Lane. The plane was damaged extensively.

Joe Norris and Dave Thomas, employees of the Soldotna Supply, were unloading lumber at the Fair home when the plane flew over at about 500 feet altitude. Shortly thereafter one of the Foster boys ran to notify them that the aircraft had crashed nearly. The Soldotna ambulance was called and the men transported to the clinic where Dr. Robert Beckman and the X-ray technician took charge.

Dr. Isaak was summoned and arrived shortly after Bowman had been flown to a hospital in Anchorage by Troy Hodges, who operates a local flying service. In his examination at the clinic, Bowman was found to have a compression fracture of the spine and possible other injuries in addition to lacerations.

After receiving treatment, Dr. Gaede was taken to his home near Soldotna where he is expected to have about a month's time to catch up on his neglected reading before returning to his practice. His injuries, in addition to lacerations of the head and face include contusions in his left shoulder, left arm and left leg and two fractured lumbar vertebrae.

While Dr. Gaede is recovering, Dr. Isaak said he and Dr. Beckman will be assisted by Dr. Peter Hansen of Juneau.

Another doctor, formerly from Seattle and now in Wrangell, Dr. Charles Hughes, also is being contacted. Dr. Hughes has expressed interest in the potential for his profession in the Kenai area.

Elmer Gaede's New Look

After the crash, it was the first time I'd see Dad in a moustache and goatee, which he grew because shaving was too painful. Even before the rest of his body mended, he was tending patients at his clinic—and shopping for another airplane.

CHAPTER 6
THE HUNTED

I STOOD AT THE VANITY of our downstairs bathroom and studied myself in the mirror. I was unimpressed. Wavy brown hair rose like a miniature tsunami atop my head. "Why don't I have straight hair like my sister, Mishal?" I thought, for the thousandth time. Then I wouldn't look like such a…dork. I had passed my twelfth birthday some months earlier and almost overnight had developed an extra measure of self-awareness, accompanied by social awkwardness. A closer examination of my reflection revealed a babyish face with blue eyes.

I'd buttoned my blue-and-brown plaid flannel shirt to the top in anticipation of venturing outdoors, where cool fall temperatures waited, along with a host of no-see-ums and white-sock flies always looking for exposed skin. Shifting my focus downward…oh, there was no downward. The image in the mirror stopped before the belt line, blocked by the vanity. I was almost a teenager and hoped for a growth spurt. But my body resolutely refused to add any additional quantity to the vertical dimension, and I remained stuck with the dubious distinction of being the shortest in my class. While I still could not pack a high-caliber rifle or shoulder a full-sized freighter packboard, those limitations didn't keep me from Alaskan adventures. In fact, Dad liked that I did not take up much space and added little weight when we flew together.

Sighing audibly, I turned away, exited the bathroom, and headed upstairs where Dad was staging gear by the front door. It was late August. Hunting season.

Hunting season marked the transition from summer vacation to another school year. Undeniably, the anticipation of hunting with Dad offset the disappointment of the inevitable confines of a classroom after a summer of unrestricted exploring. Dad must have charted my progression as a hunter, and since I had been successful in bagging a mountain goat, a moose, and a couple of caribou, in his mind, a Dall sheep was the logical next step.

Mark with Two Caribou

This hunt was for me. He had already taken a three-quarter curl sheep a mere 30-minute flight from the homestead and mounted its dramatic white head on a wall in our house, along with his polar bear and grizzly bear skins. However, for this hunt, Dad planned to hunt the western side of the Aleutian Range. This range was west of the Kenai Peninsula, across

Cook Inlet. These mountains are taller and more rugged than the Kenai Mountains, with most peaks ranging from 5,000 to 7,500 feet above the valley floors. Three volcanoes within this region exceed 10,000 feet in elevation. On the western side lies a narrow, 40-mile-long lake named Lake Clark. About midway along the lake, on the eastern shore, is a small community named Port Alsworth. It was from this community where Dad would base our hunt.

"Hey, Doc. We about ready to take off?" Dwayne King came bounding up the stairs from our basement rumpus room (later these rooms would be called "family rooms"). He and his family had just arrived in Soldotna, where he had taken a job with Missionary Aviation Repair Center (MARC), at the Soldotna airport, and needed a place to stay. Mom and Dad had an open-door, open-heart policy and never turned away a soul.

Not only did Dwayne fly for MARC, but he had volunteered to be the youth pastor at church. Our parents taught us to respect adults and to call them Mr. or Mrs.; however, in this case, we were allowed to call Dwayne by his first name—maybe because he radiated contagious energy, like a big kid, and fit into our family so well.

Now, he was eager to see what adventures the area had to offer, and the prospect of going on a hunting trip ratcheted up his enthusiasm another notch. Dad appreciated having another pilot along, especially one young enough to pack out meat.

"Come on up, Dwayne," Mom called from the kitchen. "I'm just finishing sandwiches for all of you."

"Thank you, Ruby," he responded. "You do so much for us."

"Hey, Mark. You ready for the big hunt?" he said, turning to me.

His eyes crinkled nearly shut as he grinned. He could have passed for Dad's younger brother with his wiry build and thick black hair.

I grinned back. "I sure am!"

I added my spare socks, gloves, and extra shirt to a game bag Dad had designated for the two of us. Minimizing weight and volume was critical when loading the Piper J-3, and the game bag would serve multiple functions during the hunt.

"The weather still looks good. Let's load up," Dad announced as Mom descended the stairs with a bag of sandwiches and apple slices.

This nourishment was for the first day, after which we would rely on a ring of bologna, bread slices compressed to wafer-thinness in our packs, and candy bars. In other words, standard hunting fare.

We walked to the plane and Dad started loading the gear. I did not even consider that the J-3 had only two seats for the three of us. I just waited for Dad, the loadmaster, to tell me where to sit.

Elmer Gaede with the J-3

After Dad had unceremoniously landed his blue-and-white Maule Rocket in the trees, he needed another airplane, and soon purchased an orange-and-black two-place Piper J-3. I found out later that this was the same airplane that had retrieved me from Silver Salmon Creek after Dad crashed the Maule. The J-3 was a simple aircraft. It did not have an electrical system other than the magneto, which provided the energy to the spark plugs. That meant there were no lights on the wings or inside the cabin, and no radio, much less a GPS. The instrumentation consisted of the five gauges required by the FAA for an aircraft like this: oil pressure and temperature, engine RPM, altimeter, airspeed indicator, and a compass. There were no gauges to indicate the angle of a turn, rate of climb, or where the horizon was. The fuel gauge in the nose tank was simply a cork with a piece of wire that protruded through a gas cap hole. The length of wire showing translated to the amount of fuel that remained.

Instead of a steering wheel-type yoke, common in larger airplanes, the little Piper had a stick rising from the floorboards. When airborne, pushing the stick to the side, lowered the wing in that direction, and when the pilot pushed the stick forward, the nose pointed lower; simple and intuitive. As rudimentary as this airplane was, it had several characteristics that made it a great bush plane. It was lightweight and sturdy, and the two tandem seats provided excellent downward visibility for both occupants. And, with a 90 hp Continental engine, it substantially improved performance over the stock 65 hp variant.

"Okay, Mark. You climb in first," Dad said, pointing to the back seat. "Go all the way to the back."

I placed a foot in the stirrup-shaped step, hopped inside, then eased myself over the rear seat and into the baggage compartment. Sleeping bags stacked on the aluminum frame packs and other hunting essentials comprised the "third seat." Sitting on the sleeping bags was more comfortable than the minimally cushioned rear seat, anyway. The view though, was not so good. But in my mind, I already saw a ram between the crosshairs of my rifle.

After takeoff and climbing to 5,000 feet to cross Cook Inlet, Dad held a westward heading toward the entrance of Lake Clark Pass. This particular pass through the Aleutian Range was one of the easiest passes for pilots to navigate. From the eastern approach, it runs due west for several miles before hooking sharply to the south-southwest. It remains quite wide throughout its length. The summit is only 1,500 feet, which contributes to its accessibility in all but the worst weather. Near the southern end, the pass splits around a group of razor-sharp, 7,500-foot peaks. Depending on the weather, this gives pilots two options: one side is shorter but at a higher elevation, and the other is longer but lower. The pass then terminates on the northeastern shores of Lake Clark.

Stuffed in the baggage compartment, I strained forward to see past the baseball hat that adorned Dwayne's head. Even with my limited view, I could see the glaciers hanging from the steep walls of the pass. At one point, glaciers from both sides of the pass met in the middle, completely blocking the valley. This was a fantastic sight. I watched it as long as I could before it disappeared behind us. I never imagined that fifty years later the glaciers would no longer obstruct the pass.

The 160 miles to Port Alsworth took nearly two hours. The J-3 was not very fast to begin with, and being heavily loaded didn't help. To alert people on the ground we were landing, Dad buzzed the strip at the head of the bay at Port Alsworth.

The landing gear clattered briefly when the plane touched down on the long, broad gravel airstrip. This strip was built to handle much larger aircraft, like the rugged twin radial engine DC-3. The J-3 used scarcely any of it. Dad taxied until he reached the white-and-green two-story farmhouse that dominated the small buildings at the end of the strip. Babe

Alsworth, the founder of the community, lived in the farmhouse with his wife, Mary, and their four sons. As the J-3's prop juddered to a stop, Babe came out to greet us. Like many pilots I had met, he was short and whip-thin. Hmm. Maybe my small size was an advantage when it came to being a pilot. Babe's sharp eyes watched us extract ourselves from the small Piper. No doubt he was amused by the passenger count.

The hunt was to start early the next morning, so we unpacked our sleeping bags and carried them to Babe's house where we would spend the night camped out on the floor.

"Glen, grab an extra pole for Mark and take him down to the bay," Babe instructed his youngest son. Glen, close to my age, selected two fishing poles that leaned next to the front door.

"Come on," he beckoned and headed out the door.

He handed me one of the rods, and I followed him down to the shore of the bay, a short distance from the house.

"What are we fishing for?" I asked as I examined the gear I held.

"Pike," came the clipped response.

I grinned in anticipation. I knew Glen was talking about Northern pike. I had fished for them before and took great pleasure in how they aggressively chased down a fishing lure. Their slim, torpedo shape made me think of a barracuda.

We put a bit of space between ourselves and started casting. After several retrievals, I was rewarded with a sharp tug and bent pole as a fish hit the lure. I reeled in the struggling fish. Sure enough, it was a small Northern pike, maybe 20 inches long.

"Too small to keep," commented Glen.

"I don't know what I'd do with it anyway." I laughed.

I kept my fingers clear of the razor-sharp teeth and removed the hook from its mouth before pushing it back into the bay with my foot.

"There are some a lot bigger than that," Glen said confidently.

Since he lived there, I figured he was speaking from experience.

"Keep trying?" I asked.

He shrugged his shoulders. "If you want to, but it will be time for supper soon."

A few minutes later, one of his brothers walked to the shore to bring us back to the house.

After supper, Babe, Dad, Dwayne, and I moved to the living room while Mary and the boys cleared the table. Babe had a plane on floats and Dad had arranged for him to fly the three of us to a lake at the base of the mountain the next morning, and after exchanging news stories, the discussion predictably shifted to that topic.

"Let's go back to the table," Babe suggested.

Getting up from his rocker, Babe crossed the room to the kitchen, opened the door to a cabinet, and after sorting through its contents, withdrew a map of the local area. He smoothed out the map on the recently cleared table and placed the remaining salt and pepper shakers on two corners.

The three men studied the topographical map. I wanted to get in on the conversation and leaned forward on my elbows.

Dad pointed with his finger. "Are the sheep still in that area?"

"There was a group of rams on the south and lake side of those first peaks when I flew over that area yesterday," Babe informed us. "There was a second bunch farther back in, but you don't want to go there. The country's too rough."

Dad and I had a pretty good idea of what Babe meant. Dall sheep, like other mountain sheep species, tend to stay close to nasty, nearly vertical terrain inaccessible to predators like wolves, bears…and humans. I had gotten a taste of that earlier on my goat hunts and was not eager to scare myself half-to-death again. Conversely, for Dwayne, this was his first alpine hunt, and he was itching for the experience without knowing what he was getting into.

"I figure on dropping you off about midway down the lake...right here," Babe said, pointing with a pencil. He traced a line lightly on the map.

"If you follow this draw up past the treeline, you will miss most of the alders. It is mostly birch and some spruce. From there, you can climb to the bench, which is..." He squinted at the contour lines. "...about 3,500 feet. Not a bad climb at all."

"And that's the saddle where you will drop our sleeping bags?" Dad asked.

Huh? Do...drop what? I thought. That was news to me. Dwayne didn't seem surprised. Apparently, he and Dad had discussed this.

"Yes, sir. That saddle is as flat as this table," Babe asserted, tapping the map. "They won't roll down the mountain from there. I'll take one of the boys with me to throw the gear out of the plane during the flyover."

I tuned out the rest of the details. My mind replayed the last time camping items had been tossed out of an airplane. True, it had been about five years ago, but I had not forgotten the jelly-smeared sleeping bag, the result of the glass container exploding within a dropped canister, even though Dad had wrapped a sleeping bag around it for protection from impact.

I was jarred from my reminiscing by Dad saying it was time to turn in. I slid into my sleeping bag, and despite the hard floor, I fell asleep quickly.

Babe's wife, Mary, had cooked since a young girl in fish canneries and one of her proven specialties was sourdough pancakes. She treated us to this delicious fare the next morning, after which we gathered at the shoreline where Babe had parked our transportation. Babe had several airplanes. This one was a four-place Stinson perched high on a set of pontoons. It comfortably swallowed us and our gear, with room to spare. One of the boys pushed us off. Babe keyed the starter, and the engine rumbled to life. When the engine had warmed, Babe advanced the throttle. We skimmed across the bay and into the air. Ten minutes later, we were at our destination. After the wake from the floats subsided, scarcely a ripple remained on the lake.

Usually, when we flew in a plane on floats, we wore hip boots to get to and from the plane. We did not have hip boots on this trip, but the shoreline was such that we could pull up to the beach and deplane without getting in the water.

With the hunting gear ashore, we pushed the Stinson back into the lake. Babe waved goodbye, fired up the engine, and was soon just a speck headed back from where we had come. He planned to check back later to see how our hunt was going.

I eyed our sparse stack of hunting gear: two aluminum frame packboards, game bags (some with clothes, food, and emergency gear in them), a pair of binoculars, the 8mm Mauser with the shortened stock, a box of ammo, and several hunting knives. That was about it. I may have been small for a 12-year-old boy, but my homestead activity had made me strong for my size. Still, I was not tall enough to handle an adult-sized packboard; which left me with my small Army Surplus knapsack. The binoculars and box of ammo went into my pack. Dad strapped the remaining items to the bare pack frames with generous lengths of clothesline. The lack of camping gear, which was to be dropped off up the mountain meant our packs were light. This would make our trip from where the lake sat at 400 feet elevation to the top of the saddle, relatively quick. With that expectation, we shouldered the packs. Dad grabbed the rifle, and we were off.

The late August, morning was bright and cheerful. Even without a trail, walking was easy and we made good time. Near the boggy shoreline were patches of blueberry bushes and clumps of spiny Labrador Tea. Sunshine filtered through serrated-edged birch leaves, casting an irregular pattern of shadows on the ground below. Between the staggered birch and spruce lay blankets of thick, spongy mosses. As we moved inland and the elevation increased, these plants were replaced with huddled bouquets of low willows. The previous night had been mostly clear, and dew sparkled on the foliage. As the sun rose, this scant moisture rapidly disappeared and turned back into vapor.

Dwayne could not stop talking and asking questions, and since we were several hours away from finding game, Dad responded without hesitation or trying to subdue him. As usual, I didn't say much, and instead, the flora and fauna caught my attention.

"Doc, you need a plane like Babe's," Dwayne suggested. "That way Mark wouldn't have to ride in the baggage compartment."

Dad laughed. "Well, he fit okay, didn't he?"

"Someone want to trade places on the way back?" I joked.

The two men laughed, but neither volunteered.

Dad's built-in compass led us true, and we avoided the foot-tripping, shin-bruising, pack-grabbing patches of alders in the upper reaches of the treeline and farther upslope. It was close to noon when we crested the bench. Man, had we made good time. When we topped the bench, we entered hunting mode, and our conversation was quieter. Our legs rejoiced as they recovered from the upward trek, and our backs were damp from the exertion of our rapid ascent. We dropped our packs to let the gentle north breeze dry our shirts.

Not one to stand still for long, Dad headed across the plateau. From his gait, I could tell he was measuring this patch of alpine tundra. On his return, he gave us his conclusion.

"You could almost land up here," he reported in low tones.

Dwayne whispered, "I'll bet your J-3 could do it, especially if you were light."

On my first goat hunt, at the young age of nine, I fell in love with alpine hunting and the view up here rekindled that love. The mountains petered out to the south, becoming low hills that gave out completely before collapsing on the shores of Lake Iliamna. To the east was a tumble of ragged ridges between us and Cook Inlet. To the west, was Lake Clark. The middle and southern shores were visible from this elevation, and the navy-blue water contrasted sharply with the mottled greens of the mixed forests. Here and there, I caught sight of honey-colored patches, which I knew were bogs and meadows. Port Alsworth was visible and appeared almost within arm's reach. I could see a river flowing out of the lake we had landed on and knew that returning to the community on foot was impossible. Air transport was the only way out. The perspective to the north? Wow! The slope rose gently, then quickly steepened, terminating in a citadel-like array of rank upon rank of impenetrable, nearly vertical shale. It was intimidating! It was exhilarating!

Ready to move on, Dad turned to me. "Mark, dig out the binocs."

I opened my backpack, located the binoculars, and handed them to Dad. Until now, we had not needed to scan our surroundings for game. Any sheep would have been visible on the wide-open mountainside. Their white coats would have stood out like a proverbial sore thumb against the darker greens of the alpine vegetation and the shaley rocks. But now, we would use the binoculars to peer into the spaces that had been hidden from below. We also wanted to distinguish between the rams and ewes.

We donned our packs and headed north toward the "citadel." We were not going up into that treacherous terrain but were hunting the slopes beneath it. We walked slowly, carefully now, scanning the rock-strewn tundra ahead and to both sides. The sheep could be anywhere. Before we had traveled a couple hundred yards, I spotted movement ahead. I grabbed

Dad's sleeve. We all dropped to a crouch. I pointed in the direction I had seen the motion and nodded in affirmation. It might have been just a marmot, but there had been no typical whistle of alarm. Assuming it was a sheep, we carefully dropped our packs, not letting them rattle against each other or the ground. Dad checked the magazine of the rifle to verify it was loaded but that no round was chambered. Satisfied, he handed it to me. Still crouching, we worked our way forward, Dad and I side-by-side, Dwayne a few steps behind.

We kept our eyes straight ahead toward where I had gestured. Sure enough, we saw movement again. And it was close. Grazing some 100 yards dead ahead was a group of five rams. The breeze in our faces gave us perfect stalking conditions. Though sharp-eyed, they had not seen us, and the wind kept our scent from warning them. They were completely unaware of our presence. Removing his glasses, Dad raised the binoculars. He wanted to confirm the legality of the animals ahead of us. The legal minimum was a horn size of three-quarter curl, measured from where the tip started to rise after it passed the cheek. Even with the naked eye, I could see these rams had a lot of curl. More than three-quarters. Maybe even full curl. My excitement and anticipation surged. These were trophy class animals!

"Those are *all* legal," Dad whispered. "Take your pick." A smile twitched at the corners of his mouth. I glanced at Dwayne. He looked like a boy on Christmas morning, his exuberance scarcely in check.

Lying on my belly, I inched toward a small boulder that would give me something to rest the rifle on. Once in position, I peered at the flock through the rifle's scope. I decided to take a shot at the nearest animal. Slowly, deliberately, I racked a round into the chamber and settled the butt against my shoulder. The herd remained oblivious as I steadied my aim, gradually eased the trigger back, and…BOOM! I raised my head and watched my ram drop. The others scattered then stopped…and looked around. They did not know the direction of the threat or if there even was one. Dad and Dwayne had crept up next to me, and we watched my downed sheep for signs of life. There were none. Abandoning stealth mode, we stood, and the two adults congratulated me.

"Nice shot," Dad said, patting me on the back.

That affirmation made me feel as though I had just grown a foot.

Dwayne grabbed my hand and shook it. "Yes, nice shot, Mark. Congratulations!"

We made our way to the downed animal.

Dad pulled out the hunting knives and laid them on a game bag. "Mark, that's a full curl," he said, tapping the massive horns.

I grinned until my cheeks began to cramp.

With expert ease, Dad went about dressing the ram. "Dwayne, can you give me a hand?"

Dwayne was quick to comply.

Dad kept up a monologue as the work progressed, and he sounded as though he was addressing medical school students. "When we're skinning the belly, you need to be careful not to nick the stomach. It lies just under the skin. To remove the hind quarters, we need to find the tendon that secures the leg bone to the socket. See it there?"

Dad wanted to make sure Dwayne saw what he was talking about.

I had been on enough hunts with Dad to be familiar with the procedure, which was similar, no matter the specific species. Only the size of the animal changed.

Dad distributed the meat into game bags and set aside the head with the hide down to the shoulders.

"Ah, time for lunch," announced the chief surgeon.

Our hands were bloody from dressing the sheep. We found a patch of snow nearby to clean the knives and our hands in the icy slush. Water from the snowmelt had collected at the lower end of the snow patch and served to satisfy our thirst. From my experience, some of the best-tasting water in the world drips from snowpacks.

Back at our packs, I opened the sack containing our flattened sandwiches and some apples. Had those apples been in *my* pack? No wonder it had started to feel heavy.

Lunch was winding down when we heard the drone of an airplane approaching.

"That's Babe," exclaimed Dad.

"There he is," I said, pointing slightly above the south end of the bench.

Dad made a snap decision. "Hey, we are almost ready to head down. I think we should wave him off. No need for him to drop the sleeping bags up here since we can be down at the lake before dark."

"You're the boss," stated Dwayne.

I shrugged my shoulders. I was just the boy along on the hunt, still a dad-follower.

The decision made, Dad waited for Babe to spot us and begin to circle lazily several hundred feet above us. Dad waved his arms a few times; Babe rocked the wings of the Stinson in acknowledgment, then headed back in the direction from which he had come. The plane shrunk from view and the engine drone disappeared with it.

We turned to the site of my kill. Even though we were preparing to descend the mountain, Dad kept glancing at the remaining rams, which had returned to feeding about 200 yards away, unlike typically spooked sheep that scramble to the safety of rough terrain. It wasn't the behavior of the sheep that enticed Dad, it was the size of their curls. These were larger than the one he currently had on the wall at home. I suspected that Dad was about to succumb to temptation and take one for himself. Sure enough.

"I think I'll take a shot," he said, trying to sound casual. "We can get it dressed and still be back at the lake well before dark."

Sometimes, snap decisions lead to unintended consequences. In this case, the two snap decisions would breed a multitude of such consequences.

Two hundred yards was not an exceptionally long shot for the 8mm, and Dad was a decent shot.

Dwayne and I stepped back. Dad lowered himself to his stomach and placed the rifle across one of the partially loaded backpacks. I covered my ears with my hands and locked my eyes on the sheep still grazing down range. BOOM! The shockwave slapped my chest as the round left the barrel. The rams scattered. All but one. That one went down but struggled on the mountainside. My sheep had been on a level part of the bench. Dad's struggled on a slope, enough of a slope to where…oh, oh. In its death throes, the ram went up on its side. It rolled once…. Then again… and again. It picked up momentum and kept rolling, all the way to where the slope started to flatten. Perhaps 2,000 feet down! Well, we knew the sheep was now definitely dead. Questions sprouted like weeds in the homestead garden.

"I wonder how badly the horns are beaten up?" said Dad.

"Will any of the meat be any good after that fall?" I asked.

"How are we going to get that thing back up here?" questioned Dwayne.

The issue was not a simple inconvenience. No, the sheep had rolled down the opposite side of the mountain we had climbed up. That meant we had to hike down, dress the animal, pack it back up to the bench where we now stood, and then lug both my sheep and Dad's down to the lake. Our timeline for returning to the lake shore now lay in shambles—just like Dad's sheep.

"Well," he said pragmatically, "I guess we had better go get it."

Except for a couple of game bags, the knives, and the three packs, we left everything at the kill site of my sheep. There was no need for the rifle, the binoculars, or even our extra food. We wanted to minimize the weight we would carry on our uphill labor after dressing out Dad's ram.

The descent to Dad's ram did not take long, maybe 45 minutes. Our speed was limited, not by fatigue, but by the threat of losing our footing and twisting an ankle…or worse. When we arrived at the ram, Dad took a quick survey. The horns were amazingly intact, with only a single three-inch gouge on one side. His shot had been accurate. It was just unfortunate the animal had convulsed as it had. Well, it did not matter at this point, and Dad set to dressing this second animal. This time, his butchering was hastier and less accurate.

"Shoot," I heard him mutter. I glanced over and raised an eyebrow. He just shook his head. Dwayne, who was helping Dad by holding a rear leg out of Dad's way, wrinkled his nose and turned his head away from the carcass.

Uh, huh. Nicked the gut, I thought.

Dad tossed me the quarters as he removed them, and I stripped the meat off the bones. Normally, as we had done with my animal upslope, we left the meat on the bones until it had been hung and cured back home. But, with an impending uphill climb, Dad decided to reduce pack weight by boning it right there. Boning was something I could do. I knew enough to keep the pieces of meat as large as possible so Mom and Dad would decide what to do with them later.

The sun continued its relentless arc toward the western horizon. We were on the eastern slope of the mountain, and it would go into shadow within hours and be dark by 10 p.m. Dad and Dwayne loaded up the packs. The loose meat was stuffed into game bags and secured to the packboards. My knapsack held only the knives. Dad's was the heaviest load. His pack had the horns, skin, and some of the meat. The remainder of the meat was on Dwayne's pack. It was slow going, with repetitive traversing as we worked our way uphill. We stopped frequently. As much as we knew the urgency to move during daylight, we needed to catch our breath.

Several hours later, we again crested the bench. We had climbed in shadows for nearly an hour. Now, back on top, the sun was again visible, although much lower in the sky. At least there were no clouds, clouds that would have muted our daylight more quickly.

We now set to boning my sheep quarters and redistributing the meat. The packs were looking pretty heavy.

Dad eyed the sinking sun. "We are not going to make it down before dark."

"Is that going to be a problem?" Dwayne asked. His voice registered concern.

Dad responded true to his nature, "Oh, we will be okay. We just keep going downhill until we hit the lake. Can't miss it."

I trusted Dad. He was a hunter and knew his way around mountains. We would be okay.

We worked our way along the top of the bench before dropping over the western edge, which faced the lake. I wondered if Dad and Dwayne could carry their substantially heavy packs all the way down the mountain. The packs were not "moose-hunt" heavy, but we were on a mountain, not in some flat country. They must have weighed around 100 pounds.

Since there was no trail, retracing our steps from the morning would have been pure luck, even with Dad's built-in compass. Dad picked what seemed to be the best route, and we began our winding descent. Hiking downhill may be less exerting than hiking uphill, but it takes a toll on the legs and knees, especially when supporting loads such as the two men carried. Stability was an issue, too. Maintaining balance was imperative. Otherwise, we might end up mimicking Dad's sheep. Frankly, there was no point in hurrying. We knew daylight would be gone before we reached the lake, whether we hurried or not.

Before we were completely off the flank of the mountain, the sun slid behind the Bonanza Hills on the western horizon. Our eyes adjusted as the light dimmed and we could still make out the moss and grass underfoot. We were not on the same route we had taken earlier in the day; however, we missed most of the alders. When the slope flattened, we entered the treeline, and the broken canopy above stole more of the remaining light. Our legs complained more frequently now. We said little and stopped often.

"Whew, Doc. What was that about an easy hunt?" Dwayne's good humor sounded worn down.

"What? You're not saying you're tired, are you?" Dad replied. "I think it's not that far now."

Dwayne did not know Dad like I did. Dad never got tired, or at least he never admitted it.

We were deep in the woods when we stopped to rest again. By Dad's estimate, we were still a half mile from the lake. The moon had risen, and we welcomed its pale light. Meager as it was, it painted the trees in charcoal and gray. As we stood, stooped with our hands braced on our knees to rest our backs, we heard a snap in the woods to our left.

"Did you hear that," I asked softly.

"Do you think there's a moose out there?" Dwayne's voice sounded loud.

"Could be," Dad responded.

Something in his voice did not convince me.

We stared into the woods, searching for some trace of movement. We heard another sound, like a gentle sweep of a disturbed willow. Something *was* out there. As we proceeded, our heads twisted back and forth, searching the deep shadows for clues. We heard another small crack. This time behind us. Dad and I did not verbalize the thoughts running through our heads: his and Dwayne's packs were loaded with fresh meat, and of the larger animals in the area, it was not moose that would be attracted to us. It had to be a bear, black or brown. Either way, the hunters were now being hunted. Dad chambered a round in the 8mm. The metallic snick, like an audible exclamation mark, confirmed my fear. Now, on high alert, Dad silently positioned me between himself and Dwayne. No one needed to explain to Dwayne that we were in danger, imminent danger.

In a tight, single-file line, we shuffled onward, slowly. Even with the moonlight, we could barely see what was underfoot—or what was unwaveringly hunting us. Even though I had a much lighter pack than the men, I was getting tired. I could not imagine how tired Dad and Dwayne must be now. Dad's estimated half mile to the lake had become endless. I lost track of time.

The subtle sounds continued, sometimes behind us, sometimes off to one side. Whatever it was kept its distance, an opportunist seeking an easy meal, yet held at bay by the scent of men. Who knew which would be stronger in this predator: desire or fear?

Suddenly, Dad came to an abrupt halt. I bumped into him. What did he see? The bear? But the rifle remained lowered. I shifted to one side to see around him. Small pockets of scattered moonlight rode on ripples of water just ahead. We had reached the shoreline of the lake.

This was a welcome reprieve from blindly stumbling down the mountain, but now what?

"We need to keep the meat away from where we will camp for the night," Dad said.

Our leader was tired, but he could not drop his pack and rest. Whatever was out there wanted the meat, not us. And we did not want to get between it and its desire.

Dad and Dwayne chose a spot under a tree and set their meat-laden packboards on the ground. Then we moved down the shoreline, 50 or so feet and looked for a flat spot, away from the meat. Dad had said "camp," but we had no sleeping bags; Dad had waved those off. Neither did we have a tent, not even a sheet of plastic for a ground cloth. Those items had been with the sleeping bags.

For some reason, Dad did not start a fire. Maybe he didn't have matches. More than likely, he did have matches but was too worn out to gather wood. I don't know. And why had we not heard any more sounds? When we had stopped, so had the predator. Maybe it was just watching us. I shivered, not just from the chill creeping through my jacket. I kept an eye in the direction of the tree that sheltered the meat.

The temperature had followed the sun downward, and a cloud-free night hinted at a chance of frost. Of all things, in the emergency gear bag, which I was in my backpack, was a marvel of modern technology: two space blankets. Dad handed one to Dwayne.

"Here. Open it up. We will spread one on the ground and cover up with the other one."

The sound of the men shaking the foil-colored space blankets diverted my attention and I watched them until the thin blankets flattened out. I was not impressed. I had spent a night or two under a sheet of Visqueen, and about all it did was keep the rain off my sleeping bag. Warmth had not been one of its attributes. For all I knew, when we rolled up in the new-fangled space blankets, the bear might take us for three hot dogs wrapped in tinfoil. I studied the sheep meat tree. I hoped the bear preferred Dall sheep to human sausages.

Preparing for bed was simple. Boots stayed on, even our damp clothes. Dad instructed me to crawl into the middle of the shared 5-by-7-foot "bed." Dwayne settled on one side, and Dad sat down on the other. They attempted to spread the second blanket across the top of us. Of the three of us, I was best suited for such a stingy amount of space and found myself comfortable.

Dad remained upright beside me, staring at the packs of sheep meat. I must have fallen asleep because the next thing I knew, the sky was brightening, and Dad lay snoring next to me. When he awoke, he never mentioned how long he had remained vigilant or if he had ever heard more threatening noises in the woods. I just knew we had survived the night.

Shortly after dawn, Babe flew over, splashed down, taxied to the shore and stepped onto the sandy beach. He surveyed our gear arranged on the bank.

"So, I see you got *two* sheep. I thought this was Mark's hunt."

Dad grinned lopsidedly. "I couldn't resist."

"Guess that's why you didn't make it down before dark. Nice rams, though." He pointed to our gear. "You ready to load up?"

We packed everything in and crawled in ourselves. Babe pushed the Stinson out into the lake, and we were soon winging our way to Port Alsworth.

Back at Port Alsworth, we transferred the same gear from the four-place Stinson into the two-place J-3. This took some doing. The J-3 weighed only 750 pounds when empty, and it had a load rating (useful load) of around 450 pounds. The three of us rang in at 390 pounds. Gas and oil added another 130 pounds for a total of 520 pounds, or 70 pounds over gross, and that was before we added the sheep and the rest of our gear. It was not that the well-designed Piper wing could not lift the extra weight or that the 90-hp engine could not pull it off the ground. The problem was that during even moderate turbulence or just a steep bank, the stress on the wing struts and airframe might exceed the design limits. This could cause a strut to fail and a wing to fold. In other words, a catastrophic failure.

These facts did not bother Dad, nor Babe either. No doubt Babe had flown overweight like that many times before. That was just the way bush pilots flew.

If riding in the baggage compartment had been crowded on the way over, it was about to get worse. Dad placed the bags of meat on the floor, followed by the two packboards. I lay on top of the packboards with two full-curl rams looking me in the eye. I smirked. Dwayne had a game bag of meat on his lap, no doubt in an attempt to keep the J-3's center of gravity from becoming too far aft, although no weight and balance calculations were done on this flight. He also held a sleeping bag on top of the meat, which would prove fortunate later.

Thus, neatly packaged, Dad signaled Babe to spin the J-3's prop and we were on our way.

During the two-hour flight back to the homestead, we were graced with calm winds and no turbulence. After crossing the cold Cook Inlet waters, Dad throttled back, and we started a gradual descent. Dad knew we were exceedingly heavy and treated the plane gently. At 1,000 feet we crossed the homestead. Still losing altitude, he circled to let Mom know we were back and would be landing.

The winds were calm, so he set up the approach from the north, where the trees were shorter. He crossed the threshold at 100 feet and eased the throttle back. We had plenty of runway and there was no need to hurry touchdown. I was elated! I could hardly wait to tell Mom about the hunt and show off my beautiful ram. I squirmed impatiently as Dad flared and we touched down at 45 mph. Almost there! Almost…, hey! We were turning to the left like we usually did onto the taxiway toward the house, only there was no taxiway. What was going on? What was Dad doing? Abruptly, we slammed into the fence that bordered the runway. Oof! Dwayne pitched forward, face down into the sleeping bag between him and the metal frame of Dad's seat. Even though I was wedged tightly into the baggage area, the impact banged my jaw against the back of Dwayne's seat.

After a moment, Dad opened the door and climbed out. Dwayne handed Dad the sleeping bag and the game bag of meat, then hoisted himself out. He turned to me.

"You okay back there, Mark?" he asked.

"Yeah, I'm okay." I was still in shock. When I touched my lower lip, it was already swelling. This was not how I had planned to arrive! So much for looking like a savvy hunter.

He gave me a hand and I disembarked.

Dad and Dwayne walked around the J-3 to assess the damage. The prop was bent, and one wing was wrinkled. To me, it looked like a sad, broken bird.

Mom and a family of friends, who had just arrived in Soldotna, walked up to greet us. Seeing Dad fly the J-3 into the fence must have left a less-than-admirable first impression of the bush pilot doctor.

The J-3 Crashed into the Fence on the Gaede Homestead

As it turned out, the tail wheel had become stuck in a cock-eyed position; perhaps a stone had lodged in the mechanism at takeoff. When the tail settled to the ground after touchdown it had forced the plane to the left. Because we were so heavy, the brake and rudder were not powerful enough to correct the drift into the fence. The bent prop meant the engine had to be torn down for inspection. The bent wing ended up revealing a broken wooden spar. Dad never hesitated to make the best of a bad situation and replaced the wooden spars with metal ones.

As for me, I was happy to view the mounted full-curl ram that hung on the wall next to Dad's and be reminded of another successful, thrilling hunt with Dad.

Mark's Successful Sheep Hunt

DR. ELMER GAEDE WAS ONE of several people who mentored Dwayne King into Alaska bush flying and more specifically, flying for missionary causes, such as Native Bible Camps. His abounding energy, sense of humor, and heart for people is recorded in "Open the Sky: The Story of Missionary Pilot Dwayne King," by Mark Winheld, and his current day operation can be found at www.kingdomaircorps.org.

For pictures of Port Alsworth, Babe, the Alsworth farm house, google "Babe Alsworth" or "Port Alsworth." He and Mary are also included in the digital branch of the University of Alaska-Fairbanks Oral History Jukebox project. Their legacy continues with Farm Lodge and Lake Clark Resort.

CHAPTER 7
VIEWS FROM THE BACK SEAT

AS A TODDLER IN TANANA, Dad strapped me into the back seat of the lightweight two-place Piper J-3 for quick after-work jaunts to scout for moose. When he bought a larger, four-place Piper PA-14, we set out on family outings to visit missionaries and I got to sit in first-class, upfront, on Mom's lap. My older sisters were stuck behind me in coach. When Mishal came along, I was demoted to coach, and she got the luxury of sitting beside the pilot on Mom's lap. I grew up accustomed to the sights, smells, noises, and rituals of flying in small aircraft.

When we moved to the homestead, Dad took me on airborne jaunts around the local area, as well as trips that spanned several days and covered hundreds of miles in Interior Alaska. To begin with, I learned simple things:

Small boys will likely find themselves stuffed in baggage areas along with sleeping bags or wild game meat from a fresh kill.

Praying before takeoff and invoking God's care is part of the checklist. And, in Dad's situation, absolutely necessary.

Short boys cannot see out the plane windows. They are stuck with the tedium of staring at the seat in front of them or the walls of the fuselage.

Flying in the winter entails additional planning for short daylight hours, lack of depth perception from overcast skies, and potentially blinding snow showers.

Flying in the winter requires more pilot and passenger gear, such as snowshoes, thicker clothes, double socks, heavier gloves, snow pants, and a wool hat—or in Dad's case, a hat with drop-down earflaps.

Flying in the winter demands more equipment for the airplane: wing and engine covers, and perhaps an engine heater.

A young kid may want to wait inside the warm house rather than out by the plane while his dad and his flying or hunting buddy are loading up.

Weight is a critical factor. Never carry unnecessary items. Bologna is essential. This fact should not be questioned.

Airsickness happens. Eating potato chips can be tasty and will pass the time until turbulence occurs, or there is an awareness of fumes from the nearby gas can and chamois funnel. This experience will not be forgotten, and potato chips might not be appealing for a long time afterward.

I unconsciously assimilated the above and other flying knowledge, some of which is not taught in Aviation Ground School and only learned from participation. These life-informing lessons stuck in my head and later kept me alive in the wild.

In late February or early March Dad and I were returning home from an unsuccessful caribou hunt west of Lake Clark and about 120 miles west of Soldotna. A few short years before, I would have made these journeys inside the cocoon-like confines of an Army-surplus mummy bag. Now, at age 13, and not unlike a metamorphosis, I had emerged to sit atop the rolled-up sleeping bag. The added seat cushion further improved visibility, although since the J-3 had tandem seats, I could only see out the sides of the plane; still, I was an active participant in spotting game and landmarks.

For some time, Dad and I scoured the hillsides and ice-covered lakes for caribou. Eventually, we ran out of daylight. Dad did not want to fly home and land with skis in the dark on the Gaede-80 airstrip, and since we were near Port Alsworth, he landed on Babe's snow-packed airstrip. As always, Babe and Mary invited us in for a meal and a place to sleep. Babe and Dad caught each other up on their recent flying missions and hunts, and I listened to the two bush pilots compare flight times and weather difficulties.

After supper, Babe directed me to a comfortable, high-backed chair. A full tummy, soothing heat from a crackling woodstove, and the drone of adult conversation made me drowsy, and I soon drifted off to sleep.

The next morning, Dad and I flew north along the shoreline and followed a frozen river into Lake Clark Pass. Although clouds crowded the tops of the 6,500-foot mountains that defined the pass, Dad called over his shoulder that the weather seemed nice enough. Dad had escaped many flying mishaps, and I trusted his assessment. Besides, the wind was calm. The latter was critical since the high winds that periodically raged through these mountain passes could render a small airplane unmanageable and even dash it into the mountainside.

About an hour into the flight, I leaned forward to glance beyond Dad's shoulders, and realized we were approaching the eastern end of the pass, where the mountains became hills, and the hills became marshland. I knew the marshland terminated at the waters of Cook Inlet, but something seemed wrong. Everything beyond the hills was an opaque gray. Dad eased the throttle back slightly and pushed the nose down until we were a few hundred feet above the snowy brush. In doing so, he could see beneath the low bank of clouds stacked up against the entrance of the pass. He continued toward home while I watched at close range the brush and scrubby trees glide by below.

Suddenly, Dad yanked the throttle back to idle. Again, I struggled to see past Dad, and then I understood why he had done that. Nothingness. In all the grayness, we had flown into a fogbank. With no instruments to determine the horizon, he could only hold the airplane straight and let it slowly descend to whatever was beneath us. I searched below for something to get our bearings. No brush. No trees. Void. We seemed suspended in emptiness.

Then, unexpectedly and without the slightest bump, I noticed snow spraying up from the skis. I caught my breath in astonishment. We had not crashed! We had touched down. My relief did not last. The J-3 slowed rapidly and I felt us dropping. I stiffened. Perhaps we were falling through the ice! I looked around anxiously. No water appeared behind our skis. Yet it seemed we were sinking. Subsequently, the plane stopped with a jerk. Dad advanced the throttle to full power and attempted to taxi. The J-3 did not budge. We were stuck. At least we were down in one piece. I sat stock-still. Dad switched off the magnetos and the prop shuddered to a stop. He unsnapped his seatbelt and turned around to me, "We might as well get out for a bit until the fog lifts." He stated this as though it had been a routine landing.

"Okay," I agreed. He was my dad, a bush pilot who had survived other emergency landings in blizzards on narrow shorelines. He had experience. He did not seem alarmed. He would figure out what to do.

I watched him climb out and stand briefly on a ski. His next step let me know he was writing another story. Heavy, wet snow swallowed him up to his waist. No wonder we couldn't taxi. The 90-hp motor could not overcome the drag of the glue-like snow.

Dad surveyed our new predicament and announced, "I guess we will have to tromp out a runway so we can take off. Can you dig out the snowshoes?"

I reached into the long, narrow cargo area behind the rear seat and produced two pairs of wooden snowshoes: long-tailed, traditional ones for him and bear-paw ones for me. The thermometer on the airplane side window read 34 degrees F, warmer than expected, and since we anticipated heavy exertion, we shed our coats and left them in the airplane.

After strapping on the snowshoes, we plodded away from the airplane, leaving two parallel sets of tracks the width of the airplane skis. It was not easy going. The snow stuck to our snowshoes, just as it had to the skis on the airplane, and it was deep. Even with snowshoes, we had to raise our feet six to eight inches to take a step. We labored for a half-hour, occasionally looking back to make sure we packed the snow in a straight line.

"How much runway do you think we have? Five hundred feet?" Dad asked.

I was just a young teenager and not yet good at judging distances. I felt like we had gone a mile. I shrugged my shoulders.

"It could be," I ventured. Inwardly, I felt pleased he'd asked my opinion.

We toiled another 100 feet and then turned around and stomped back to the airplane. The fog had lifted enough for us to make out a line of trees three or four hundred yards to the north. There were still no landmarks visible to the south or ahead to the east, but the weather was improving, although still not good enough to risk a takeoff. We climbed back into the plane.

"I was hoping to get back in time for church," he mused.

He scanned the clouds intently as if he could part them by sheer willpower. He would have been outside pacing if the snow had not been so deep.

My stomach growled. His did, too. He pulled out two plain Hershey's chocolate candy bars and handed one to me. I would have preferred a Snickers with a layer of caramel and nuts. Dad, however, had informed me that when a person worked hard, nuts interfered with breathing; accordingly, he vetoed my preference. I tore off one end of the wrapping and inspected the contents suspiciously. Dad did not refresh his emergency gear chocolate bars. Though I had no proof, I suspected some might have even dated back to my birth year. After a myriad of freeze-thaw cycles, they appeared to be dipped in flour. The one I opened, however, did not appear leprous; therefore, it must have been of relatively recent vintage. Besides, I was hungry.

After what seemed like ages, the sky brightened, the fog dissipated, and we could see that the line of trees, about a mile away, curved in front of us.

"Looks like we are on a river," remarked Dad.

The weather continued to improve, and we could see definition in the smooth layers of the stratus above us.

"Let's give it a shot," Dad said, eager to move on.

Typically, when a plane on skis is preparing to taxi, the pilot or passenger gets under a wing, grabs hold of the strut at the point closest to the wingtip and rocks the wings up and down. This movement breaks the skis loose from the snow. In this case, the snow was too deep, and Dad could not push up on the strut, without sinking deeper into the snow The wings would not have rocked at all.

As for me, I could not reach the top of the strut, even when standing on hard-packed snow. I couldn't help at all. The other issue was starting the engine. Dad had to stand on a ski and grab the prop from behind. He used this same method when the airplane was on floats; however, it was more awkward on the snow-covered skis. Fortunately, the warm engine started easily, and after a quick engine RPM check, Dad glanced over his shoulder to make sure I had my seatbelt on.

"Ready, Mark?"

I nodded.

Satisfied we were prepared to launch he advanced the throttle to full power. The plane did not move. The engine strained. The airplane vibrated. All to no avail. I wondered if we might end up spending the night at this spot.

Dad did not give up. Still at full power, he worked the rudder pedals in an effort to get the tail of the airplane to wag back and forth. This was another method to break the skis loose. After a couple of attempts, it worked.

We started to slide along our packed-down path. Would our snow-shoed runway be long enough? Would we end up stuck again? I willed the airplane to go faster.

The J-3 normally popped into the air quickly. Not this time. The gummy snow was stubborn. I watched the end of our packed path disappear behind us. We still had not gained enough speed to become airborne. The trees ahead came into sharper view. Could we get into the air before hitting them? Dad was not out of options. He pushed the stick to the right to try and break one ski free of the tacky snow and reduce the overall drag. Pilots used this technique when taking off on floats, which also worked on skis. To my relief, and I'm sure his, too, the trick worked. With one ski free, the airplane picked up speed rapidly and we soon climbed higher and higher to reach a safe altitude to cross Cook Inlet and get back home.

One Sunday afternoon the next February when I was 14, Dad decided to shoot some landings in preparation for another upcoming caribou hunt. Pilots would typically seek out local environments similar to where they planned to hunt and "shoot," or practice, landing on those surfaces. He asked if I wanted to go along. I immediately agreed. Daylight hours were brief at this time of year, and after finishing our traditional after-church Sunday dinner of fried chicken and mashed potatoes, we had only a few hours before the sun would retreat. Dad would never have considered skipping church—or Sunday dinner—to go flying, and now, he figured the amount of time would be adequate.

After several weeks of unseasonably warm weather, much of the snow on the Kenai Peninsula had melted. When the cold returned, temperatures sank to near zero. The afternoon sun struggled to melt the sparkly frost off the wings, and Dad had set up a heater to warm the J-3's engine. He planned to fly 15 minutes east of the homestead to a cluster of small lakes between Soldotna and Skilak (SKEE-lak) Lake. Since this was such a short hop, aside from the emergency gear that was always on the plane, there was no need for extra clothes, a tent, or other emergency items. It would be an afternoon outing, not a hunt or cross-country flight. Dad had selected an area near Skilak to practice landings because the environment was similar to where we planned to hunt later. The Piper J-3 started readily and shortly thereafter skated down our icy runway, lifted off, and headed east.

The topography is relatively flat between our homestead and Skilak Lake, with a few low hills, a pattern of swamps, insignificant lakes, scattered clumps of black spruce and aspen, and a few meandering streams. As usual, Dad flew at 500 feet to look for moose, not that they were in season, but it was a habit pilot-hunters had acquired. The wind had swept clean the lake surfaces and the ice appeared dark with a rim of snow around the edges, not unlike a monk's haircut. Dad could have landed on any of them, although bush pilots knew there was a downside. Without friction on the glare ice to slow the airplane, it would be difficult to stop. An idling propeller alone was often enough to keep the aircraft traveling forward. Despite this complication, Dad chose one to land on.

He descended cautiously and touched down lightly on a half-mile-long lake. I always watched the gear whenever we landed, whether on skis, wheels, or floats, and observed how deep floats settled into the water, how wheels sank into the sand, and how skis made a mark in the snow. In this case, I was watching the skis. Dad angled toward the shoreline; confident the plane would slow to a stop.

Then I saw what he did not, because his focus was forward. Cracks were starting to spread from behind the skis. First one, then two. Then a spider's web worth! My pulse quickened and I prepared for the inevitable. We were going to fall through the ice! Like most Alaskan kids, I did not know how to swim. There was only a short summer interval when local lakes were marginally warm enough to attempt lessons. And, you had to be willing to offer your body up to clouds of mosquitoes. Learning to swim was not high on people's lists. Not only that, while I wore a flotation device when in the float plane, I never wore one when the plane was on skis. Why should I? My terror heightened and I gasped. The J-3 had high wings. If we fell through the ice, the wings would probably stay on top, blocking our escape. The thought of getting trapped was one of my worst nightmares.

Panicked, I pounded on Dad's shoulder.

"Dad! Dad!"

When he turned, I pointed to the cracks zigzagging like lightning from the skis. He immediately went to full power. Too late. The ice gave way, and we sank. Water sprayed. Ice flew. Dad kept the throttle to the firewall but to no avail. Our forward progress stopped. We slowly descended into the icy water. I gripped the back of Dad's seat and expected to see water entering the cabin. It didn't. Dad shut down the engine. We sat motionless, without speaking. What was going on? Finally, Dad opened the clamshell door and looked over the side.

"Looks like overflow," he commented calmly.

I leaned over to see for myself. Although I sensed Dad's optimism, I was not convinced this story would end well.

The upper layer of ice we had fallen through was about an inch-and-a-half thick, not enough to hold up the airplane. I wondered how thick the ice below it was. My pessimistic pondering abruptly ended when Dad climbed out of the front seat. He braced himself on the wing strut and swung onto the thin ice. The ice held his 150-pound weight. Even at age 14,

I was not even close to 100 pounds. Surely, the ice would hold my weight too. I duplicated his acrobatic maneuver and stood beside him on the thin ice. The airplane rested in over a foot of water...and we were not equipped for water operations. We had on warm snow boots, not hip boots. These were waterproof but made for snow, not wading in water.

When the sun dipped below the horizon dropped below zero. Icy fingers formed across the open water where we had fallen through, preparing to seal the ragged wound extending behind the J-3.

"Maybe we can get some logs under the nose of the skis and get them back up on the ice," Dad suggested.

Although I had rapidly recovered from my terror, I still would have preferred being off the thin ice.

On the shoreline, less than a hundred feet away, lay dead trees of various sizes, reminders of a forest fire decades ago. We slid our way to the shore, sorted through the debris, and carried a few smaller logs back to the stranded airplane.

"Do you think you can lift a wing so I can slip a log under the ski?" Dad questioned.

"I think so," I replied.

"Let's start with the left side," he said.

I nodded. Staying standing on the extremely slick ice required attentiveness. I kept my weight centered over my boots and shuffled over to the left wing. Fortunately, since the airplane sat low in the water, I could reach the upper section of the wing strut and still have enough height to lift. I was plenty strong, just pitifully short. Dad knelt at the edge of the ice next to the left ski, slid the end of a log into the water, and prepared to shove it under the nose of the ski as I lifted the wing. He gave a nod, and I heaved upward. The wing lifted. My sense of relief turned to concern as the ice I stood on began to crack and sag. I was not afraid of drowning in this shallow area but getting wet with no way to dry off or warm up could be just as deadly. I immediately let the wing settle back down. Besides, I had not raised the wing high enough anyway for Dad to slide the log under the ski.

"This isn't going to work," he said. "The water is too deep. We need to get closer to shore."

He took off his wool hat and scratched his head. I could tell he was looking for potential solutions. "Grab that short log over there and help me break the ice in front of the skis."

I caught on to what he was thinking. We were going to break the ice so he could taxi toward the shore, where the overflow was not as deep and the ice on top was thicker.

I grabbed a four-foot section of a three-inch diameter log.

"I'm ready," I said.

Together, we shattered the ice and soon cleared a slushy path to where the water was only a few inches deep. Dad headed back to the plane while I stayed on the shore.

Back at the plane, Dad hung onto the wing strut and swung into the front seat. A moment later, he stepped back onto the gear leg step and leaned forward to grab the prop. He pulled the prop downward, and the engine spun to life. While the engine warmed up, he pulled the door shut, knowing the prop blast would spray water everywhere when he throttled up.

I watched from the shoreline, hoping this would work–and soon. We needed to get back home. My face felt chilled, and a shiver ran down my back. If we did not get out of here shortly, we would need to start a fire to stay warm. Dad advanced the throttle, and the J-3 began to move.

"It's working!" I yelled, clapping my hands even though no one could hear me.

He carefully guided the airplane down the narrow waterway. Upon reaching the end, he switched off the engine.

"Let's lift and swivel the plane to get the skis up on the ice one at a time," Dad proposed.

"What about the tail?" I asked, thinking it would hit the unbroken ice and keep the plane from rotating.

He glanced at the back of the airplane.

"You're right," he said approvingly. "Let's break the ice around the tail, so it's free to move."

From that point, we rapidly made headways. With one ski on the ice and thicker ice to stand on, it was simple to revolve the remaining ski onto a solid footing. Now that the airplane was secure, Dad had to once again prepare for flight. A sheen of ice covered the tail section where the prop blast had sprayed it, and we gently chipped it off. Dad also made sure all the control surfaces moved freely. Finally, he deemed the airplane airworthy.

"Okay. Climb in," he told me.

I placed my foot in the stirrup step for the rear seat and nearly fell on my face. The prop blast had covered it in ice when Dad taxied to the shore. I tried again, keeping a firm grip on the side of the door frame, and pulled myself in. Dad switched the magnetos on and stepped around the front of the J-3 to spin the prop. The engine started and I snugged up my seatbelt as Dad climbed back in. He fastened his seatbelt, pulled the door shut, and pushed the throttle forward. The airplane hugged the snow-covered beach edge as Dad guided it in a safe line. Within 150 feet, we were airborne and headed home.

Landing on the homestead in the retreating daylight was uneventful, and after we tied the faithful little airplane in its parking spot, we walked through the peaceful dusk to the house. Well, "peaceful" until we stepped inside.

Mom was standing at the top of the bi-level stairs, apron tied around her waist, flour on her face, and hands on her hips. She had heard Dad buzz the house like he always did when he returned from flying, and was waiting to see us walk through the door—safe and sound.

"You're late…what happened?" she demanded anxiously. With Dad's track record of flying near-casualties, she had every reason to be concerned.

Dad sat silently on the bottom step with his back to her and untied his boots.   I looked up at Mom. "We fell through the ice," I announced with a gleam in my eye. Hey, we had made it home. We'd survived. I bet I'd be part of Dad's stories the next time he and Mom entertained Sunday dinner guests.

Before Mom said a word, I kicked off my boots and ran downstairs to my room. Behind me, I heard her voice again.

"Elmer!"

From the back seat, not only did I learn critical bush flying techniques, I learned about my dad.

He never showed fear or panicked.

He was forever practical and resourceful.

His eternal confidence amazed me.

He trusted his airplanes.

Later, I became aware of how much he pushed the limits of flying, but for now, I expected he would find a way out of any predicament, even if those experiences caused moments of panic for me.

CHAPTER 8

ECHO LAKE:
FIRE AND ICE

I STOOD AT THE PICTURE WINDOW in our living room. Its 5-by-7-foot opening provided a panoramic view of our front yard, driveway, and the road ahead of our house. It still got dark this time of year, and tonight, I watched the pulsing orange glow of the forest fire a mile to the east. Thick spruce trees, like we had on our homestead hid the flames and I could not see the actual fire. Dry spruce trees. The glow suddenly intensified. Another stand of trees must have been engulfed. Very dry trees. I wondered if our homestead would burn tonight.

The spring of 1969 had been unusually dry. The lack of April showers could not be blamed for our absence of May flowers since we never had May flowers anyway. Dandelions did not count. But the drought, which began in April and continued into May, was responsible for the area-wide threat of forest fires. After a protracted, frigid winter, we were thrilled to see the snow and ice melt. The rivers and streams were just waking up and not close to their summer levels yet, but the land seemed to stretch and yawn in preparation for the explosion of summer. But it was not summer. Yes, the snow was gone, but no trace of green freshened the dullness. In open areas, dead grass from the previous year lay like mats of tinder waiting for a spark. The aspen trees were still leafless. Undergrowth was still dormant. Yes, it was dry.

Then on May 23, a mere half mile from our homestead, across Echo Lake Road, a match was struck and a burn barrel lit. Heat from the burning trash carried a scrap of burning paper skyward. It spun lazily and finally settled into a ditch choked with dry grass. The tinder exploded, and the fire, fanned by an easterly breeze, quickly spread. A gust of wind carried a burning blade of grass across Echo Lake Road where it ignited more grass. From there, it spread into the woods and quickly into the trees themselves. It was now a forest fire.

School had ended the previous week, and I was in no rush to get out of bed. It was the time of year when summer was so close yet seemed far away. There was no point in pedaling my bike down gravelly, bumpy Gas Well Road to Slikok Creek. No fish had found their way back and the adjacent gravel pits were barely free of ice. There were no frogs to hunt or swallows to chase. Life had not awakened.

As much as I wanted to ride my Honda motorbike on the runway, in shady areas, like the taxiways, the ground remained soft and muddy because the remaining frost beneath it had not thawed. Even if I didn't bury my bike in the muck, I knew Dad would be noticeably upset with any ruts he found. I could hear him say, "I see your bike left some deep tracks on the taxiway. Go out there and smooth them out."

After a while, I grew tired of checking to see if the pools of water had finally disappeared, and solid ground had reappeared. Some days, I wished I had a dove to release from my basement window to search for dry land and fly back with a report. It had worked for Noah.

The sun had already been up since 5 a.m. and daylight sneaked around the gaps between my window and the pull-down shade. I stretched and swung my legs over the side of the bed. My feet landed on a pile of clothes I had shed unceremoniously the night before, and I reached for my jeans and shirt before heading upstairs to forage for breakfast.

The homestead routine had been in shambles the prior two weeks, with Mishal and I fending for ourselves. Naomi had not arrived home from college. Mom and Dad had flown Outside (word used for any place outside of Alaska, typically the Lower 48 States) to attend Ruth's boarding school high school graduation ceremony in Oklahoma, after which Mom stayed behind to visit her folks in Kansas.

It was not as though we were left in the wilds on our own. Dwayne King and his family had moved into our cabin and Mom and Dad had asked them to look in on us from time to time; although Dwayne frequently flew in and out of Interior villages with his work for MARC and wasn't always around.

At least Dad and Ruth had returned to the homestead a few days before, but even then the house still did not feel right. Mom's household management and nurturing were missing, as were the sounds of her making breakfast in the kitchen. Good thing I knew how to dump cold cereal in a bowl, splash some milk on it and throw a slice of bread in the toaster. I was 13. I could handle this.

After gulping my cereal, a trait I'd learned from Dad, I rinsed my empty bowl and left it in the drain rack. I grabbed a second piece of toast, smeared on margarine, trotted down the steps, and out the front door.

I had not seen Dad yet. I knew he rose earlier than me on most Saturdays, and I expected to find him in the hangar repairing something. When I stepped onto the circle drive, I noticed that even though Mom's red Chevy Impala was there, Dad's white Saab was missing. I figured he must have gone to the clinic to deliver a baby, or maybe two. Some women seemed to wait until he was back in town before allowing their babies to be born.

Beyond the hangar was our red-roofed barn. The upper loft rested on log walls, and Dad had finished the gable ends in rough-cut 1-by-6 siding, milled from spruce, which he and Mom had cut down to clear the runway. We had two horses, and I guessed Ruth might be out there. After being gone for the school year, she seemed almost like a stranger now. I needed to get reacquainted.

The Homestead Barn

Sure enough, there she was, outside the corral beyond the barn with her horse, Penny, a stocky pinto, tied to the top log of the fence with a lead rope.

"What are you doing?" I asked.

She turned to acknowledge me. "Oh, hi, Mark. I'm checking Penny to make sure her feed is okay and maybe brush her a bit."

I was glad Ruth was back, if for no reason other than I did not have to carry buckets of water to the barn daily. I wondered why Ruth thought she needed to brush Penny. Since her return, she had groomed Penny every day, and Penny's coat was already smooth and glossy, her winter coat brushed away.

Ruth with Penny and Penny's Foal Koko

"Do you know where Dad's at? The car's gone."

"He's in town."

"Oh, okay."

I turned around, moseyed back toward the house, and stopped at the barn to see if I could spy some black-and-blue blowflies. Sometimes, they warmed themselves in the sun on the gable ends. Maybe I would get my BB gun and plink a few. I was accustomed to larger guns, like .22s, the 8mm Mauser, and even Dad's .300H&H, but those were definitely overkill for shooting flies, not to mention dangerous. Bullet holes punched in the gable end would not have gone over well, either. Today, it didn't matter anyway. There were no flies out sunning.

Next, I searched for Mishal. When Mom and Dad left on their trip Outside, Mishal and I declared a ceasefire from our incessant squabbling. I was curious to see if the truce was still in place. As I reached the house, she flew out the front door. The screen door banged behind her. She headed for the woodshed, off the south end of the house. I flagged her down.

"Mishal!" I yelled.

She paused and turned to face me.

"What do you want?" she spat.

So much for the truce, hostilities simmered just beneath the surface.

"What are you going to do?"

"I'm going to ride my bike."

"Oh."

Our bikes were old, used ones that Mom or Dad had picked up somewhere. We parked these bicycles wherever we were when we grew tired of pedaling. She had ditched hers in the woodshed; mine was in the hangar. I sprinted to get mine. Maybe I could talk her into a race. I grabbed my bike's handlebars, kicked up the kickstand, and pushed off, down the driveway and past Dad's J-3, tied at the road's edge. It looked like it was waiting for my dove to return with an olive branch and pronounce the runway safe to use again, too; until then, it would have to take off and land on the road. I turned toward Gas Well and saw Mishal riding a short distance away.

"Wait up!" I hollered at her back.

She ignored me and kept going. I pedaled faster and closed the distance between us. When I caught up, she performed a hasty U-turn and headed back the other way. Sisters! I turned around in front of the cabin and noticed there was no car out front. Maybe Dwayne was up flying. Maybe his wife and children had driven into town. It didn't matter now anyway; Dad had returned from Outside. I continued back to the house and found Mishal doing laps around our driveway. I pulled up next to her.

"Wanna race?"

"No."

"I'll win, you know."

"Leave me alone."

I stood on my pedals, accelerated past her, and continued around the driveway.

On the next lap, I hit my brakes and slid to a stop. Above the trees to the east was what looked like a dark cumulus cloud. Only it was too dark. And it moved too rapidly. *That* was smoke. Lots of smoke!

Mishal stopped to see what had caught my attention.

"Go to the house!" I shouted.

She didn't argue with me. I pedaled as fast as I could to the barn.

"Ruth, Ruth! There's a fire!"

I dropped my bike, and we ran to the house together. I could now see flames mixed with the smoke. The fire was huge, and it was close!

Wide-eyed, Ruth stared at the smoke. "What do we do?" I could hear the panic in her voice.

Except for Naomi, none of us siblings had take-charge personalities, and now Mom and Dad were not here to tell us what to do. Even though Ruth was the second oldest, she stood frozen. Out of urgency and by default, I made a decision.

"We have to leave the homestead. We have to leave NOW!"

The words were like a knife in my stomach. This was home. How could we leave? We broke into a frenzy.

"Get some things and throw them in the back of the Impala!" I yelled.

Ruth was frantic. "Where are the keys?"

"What do we take?" shrieked Mishal.

"Grab some clothes!" I hollered.

"Oh, no! The horses!" Ruth turned toward the corral.

"Ruth! We don't have time!" I barked out orders, unbecoming of my typically deferring personality.

I ran upstairs, darted into Mom and Dad's bedroom, grabbed an armful of clothes from their closet, bounded down the stairs, through the door, and into the yard where the red Chevy waited. The rear driver's side door was open, and I threw in the clothes. Then I sprang around to run inside for another load, nearly colliding with Ruth, who had her own bundle. Mishal had disappeared downstairs to find some of her things. I followed her, ran into my room, and located my most valuable possession: the mounted goat skin pinned to the wall beside my bed. Wildly, I tore it from the wall, bounded back up the steps, and threw it on top of the pile of clothes. With the smoke moving closer, I shot back inside and snatched the Chevy keys from inside the closet.

"Ruth! I have the keys! Let's go! NOW!" I couldn't believe I was ordering my older sister around.

And where was Mishal? "Mishal, we have to leave. GET UP HERE!"

Outside, I could hear the rumble and crackle of the fire. I knew a bit about fires since I had worked with Dad, cutting trees, and burning the slash. I knew the painful heat of a powerful blaze. This was magnitudes greater, and seeing the raging inferno, I wondered if this was what hell was like.

Ruth slid behind the wheel and started the Chevy. Mishal appeared with a bulging pillowcase, tossed it in the back seat, ran to the car's front passenger side, and scrambled inside. I slammed the rear car door and raced around to join my sisters in the front seat. Ruth had the Impala moving even before I yanked the door shut. She started down the driveway.

"Go left, left!" I screamed.

She hesitated.

"The fire is too close to the road! We need to go out the back way!"

There were essentially two ways off the homestead: Gas Well Road to the right and the road past the Herrs' to the left. This second road was definitely the road less traveled. No one maintained this narrow gravel road, and bicycle and motorbike traffic by us neighborhood kids were its primary use. It wound through the woods until it ended in a gravel pit. From my forays there, I knew a rutted path edged around the pit and would get us to West Poppy Lane, then back onto Kalifonsky Beach Road, from where we could drive to Soldotna.

Ruth obeyed, turned left, past the J-3, and headed toward Herr's. I looked back toward our homestead, and while I did not turn into a pillar of salt, I froze at the sight of the towering billows of smoke. I did not want to forget any detail. Inside, I sobbed. I truly believed this would be the last time I'd see the homestead unburned.

We passed the Herrs'. The boys were out in the yard, staring at the clouds of smoke. The road tapered. Ruth glanced at me.

"It's okay. Keep going," I urged her.

I started a monologue. "There's a soft spot in the dip around this corner. Don't slow down. Watch the alders on the corner. There's the gravel pit. No! Don't go down into it... stay to the left. See the trail now? To the right...there."

"That's the trail?" Ruth was doubtful. She could ride her horse down that, but would the Impala make it?

"It's okay. Really. Dad drove through here in the Saab once."

Now that I thought of it, maybe that was where he had broken the tire rim.

The trail was wide enough for the car but rough. Mishal and I hung on as the Chevy bumped and bounced for a hundred yards. Then, it bottomed out on the approach to West Poppy. Tires spun. The steering wheel sawed back and forth as Ruth herded the Impala up the shoulder and onto the gravel road. From there, it was less than a quarter mile to Kalifonsky Beach Road, where we could get to town.

"Where should we go?" Ruth blinked back tears.

We did not know where Dad was, just that he was in town.

"Maybe go to the airport...the fire can't get us there," I said.

I shook from the drama of our escape.

Ruth tried to dab at her eyes and hang onto the steering wheel. "Okay. Then we need to find Dad."

Ten minutes later, Ruth pulled to a stop in front of the MARC hangar, and we exited the Chevy, clustering together before we approached the entry. We did not want to be separated. I pushed open the door to the office, and in a clump, we stepped across the threshold. We recognized many of the people, including the matronly receptionist.

"Well, hello!" she greeted us with a warm smile. "It's nice to see you children. May I help you with something?"

"There's a fire...and...we need to find Dad," Ruth explained haltingly.

"Oh! I'm sorry. Is everyone okay? You can use the phone if you would like." She did not wait for a response and set the phone on the counter so Ruth could reach it.

The clinic was the obvious place to check. In the commotion to escape the threat of fire, we had not had time to call from the house, besides, our phone was on a party-line and who knows if we would have been able to get through.

Ruth dialed the clinic number. I prayed Dad would answer. Ruth stood there, phone against her ear. I held my breath. Then.... "Dad, Dad! There is a fire by the homestead, and we.... Oh, this is Ruth."

There was a pause.

"Yes, we are at the airport. We didn't know what to do!"

Another pause.

"Yes, all three of us."

Yet another pause, then...

"Okay."

Ruth hung up the phone. "Dad's coming."

I nearly collapsed with relief. Dad was coming. It would be okay.

The hangar staff gathered outside the open hangar door and looked west to the towering clouds of smoke. About 15 minutes later, Dad arrived. We dashed outside and flocked around him, all talking at once.

"We were so scared!" blurted out Mishal.

"We grabbed some clothes. But didn't know what else to bring," added Ruth.

"It happened so fast!" I exclaimed.

Dad regarded each of us as he digested our jumbled and emotionally laden repeated sentences.

He processed quickly and had a plan. I knew he would. He walked over to the men in front of the hangar door, with us at his heels. We were not about to lose Dad. Following a brief conversation, he turned to us.

"Ruth, you and Mishal stay here while Mark and I go check the homestead. I'll call MARC when it's safe to come home. Wait in the office lounge. I'll take you inside."

We returned to the office. The kindhearted receptionist walked slowly around the counter, put an arm around each girl, and soothingly ushered them to a side room with a couch and coffee table.

"I heard the men talking. You can stay here as long as you need to. We'll take good care of you. Can I get you something to drink or a little snack? I bet she had homemade cookies tucked away, like she did at her house. I always felt special when our family visited her. She would pull me aside and whisper, "Mark, I think you need one more cookie, don't you?" I had no doubt she would comfort my sisters. I wondered if they would save me a cookie.

Dad thanked the receptionist, and we stepped outside. He opened the driver's door of his white Saab. "Let's go."

I climbed into the front seat and we headed home.

Present Day Map of the Homesteads, Roads, and Location Where the Fire
Started on Echo Lake Road, a Half Mile from the Gaede Homestead

When we reached the intersection of Gas Well and Kalifonsky Beach Road, we found Gas Well blocked by sawhorses. A State Trooper manned the barrier. Dad rolled down his window and was immediately recognized.

"Headed home, Dr. Gaede?" the Trooper asked.

Dad nodded and the Trooper moved aside the barrier. We drove past Echo Lake Road, where remains of once tall green spruce stood black and smoldering. Smoke billowed off to the southwest, still close but not toward our homestead. This was encouraging. We turned down the road to our house. Dad stopped by the J-3 and got out.

"Let's go take a look. Untie the wings. I'm going to go get my camera."

I soon had the wings free. Dad sprinted back to the plane, and I followed him around as he did the preflight. He moved the ailerons, checked a safety wire on the hinges, moved the tail surfaces, and finally drained a bit of gas from a settling bowl beneath the engine.

"Hop in, Mark."

I complied and once seated, fastened my safety belt.

Dad spun the 90-hp engine to life, climbed into the front seat, secured himself, and taxied out on the road. Soon we were airborne.

He had taken off to the north, putting the fire behind us. He now turned 180 degrees, and in less than a minute we were skirting the front edge of the inferno. From an altitude of 500 feet, I could see the flames climbing the spruce and leaping from one to the next. Small fires started ahead of the leading wall of flame, where embers had been carried and pushed forward by the east wind. The fire seemed alive, intent on devouring every living thing in its path. Inside the cockpit, I smelled smoke. Dad turned steeply to make another pass. I did not feel as afraid up here. The fire could not reach us, and we could outrun it. I just wished Dad didn't fly so close to it. Then, satisfied he had enough pictures, Dad turned toward our homestead just a half mile away.

Echo Lake Fire in the Background and the Gaede's
Chevy and Saab in the Forefront

139

Back on the ground, Dad tied down the J-3.

"I think we are going to be okay," he said. "The wind is carrying the fire to the southwest and we have Gas Well Road as a firebreak. I will call Ruth and tell her to come home."

When Ruth arrived, Dad helped us unload the Impala. I could not tell if he was amused or perplexed by what we had collected, especially when he pulled out the goat skin.

"Uh, I'll take that," I mumbled.

I gathered up my prized possession and hurried down to my bedroom. Putting that back on the wall would take more effort than it had to tear it off.

Ruth put together a simple supper something we were familiar with: grilled bologna and cheese sandwiches. Dad could have lived on bologna, whether at home or when hunting. With Ruth puttering around the kitchen, it felt a bit like Mom was there. Whereas Dad provided direction and strength for our family and was the framework, Mom's presence was the glue that held our home together.

I nibbled at my sandwich, distracted. I wanted to leave my chair and stay, like a sentinel, at the living room window, scanning the sky for smoke. I had already left my seat twice, earning a questioning look from Dad.

Dad finished his supper before the rest of us and laid out the plan for the evening.

"Ruth, you water and feed the horses as usual. Mishal, help Mark wash the dishes. Put them away after you dry them. I'm going to gas up the J-3."

I watched him sit on the bottom step of the stairs and tie his shoes. What had I done to deserve kitchen duty? I should be outside helping gas up the airplane. Maybe I should not have grabbed my goat and taken it along. Sigh.

Outside, the spigot squeaked as Ruth filled two galvanized buckets.

I turned to my own chores. "Mishal, please help me clear the table. Can you put the pickles back in the fridge?"

The fear and chaos of the day made the need for mutual support stronger than our sibling rivalry, and for the moment, we were good friends.

"Do you want to wash or dry?" I asked.

"I'll dry."

It did not take long to finish the supper dishes. Ruth had completed her tasks as well. She called from the basement. "Mishal come pick up your half of the room."

Mishal groaned and sauntered down the steps without any urgency. She and Ruth shared a bedroom and had very different opinions on order and tidiness. The hasty departure of the morning had not helped, and I imagined clothes strewn everywhere. From what I heard coming from their room, it was not going well. I was glad I had my own room.

I again went to the living room window and saw Dad on his way in. Back in the house, he settled into his recliner and shook open a newspaper. While he caught up on yesterday's news, I laid on the floor, chin cupped in my hands and kept a vigil. I did not trust the fire. Dad finished his scan of the paper and picked up his black, leather-bound Bible. It was Saturday night, and he might have been preparing to teach a class the next day. Or maybe he was reading about Noah…and the dove. After a while, I stood up. It was starting to get dark. I studied the sky before me one more time.

"Dad, I'm going to take my bath."

It was, after all, Saturday, the day when all the dirt of the week was washed away, like a good confession. I knew the chances were slim of finding the only bathroom downstairs unoccupied, but at least I could make my intentions known to my sisters.

Sure enough, when I arrived, the door was shut and light showed past the crack under the door. I did not bother to knock but continued directly to my bedroom. I switched on my reading light, grabbed a paperback book from my nightstand, and flopped on my bed.

With my head against my pillow, I regarded my assortment of plastic model airplanes hanging from the ceiling. I grimaced. They were in disarray, pointed in unusual altitudes, and one was even inverted. Ripping the goat skin off the wall had created havoc in the skies above my bed. At some point, this disruption would have to be addressed. Not now. I was too tired from the day's upheaval. Instead, I started to read. Like many other books precariously stacked on my nightstand, the book was about a WWII fighter pilot. This one flew Spitfires. I had just turned a page when Dad stuck his head around the corner.

"I'm going to go check on the fire."

I padded upstairs to my lookout, the picture window. The white Saab disappeared in the direction of Gas Well Road. I remained at the window, and in the failing daylight, I searched the east. Then I saw it. A flicker of orange above the trees. Now, it had my full attention. More flickering. Several minutes passed. Dad was not back. I chewed my lip. Daylight continued to fade as one source of light gave way to another. At first, I thought the glow was reflected off clouds, but then I realized it was reflected by smoke. The fire was raging again. Maybe it had jumped Gas Well and was headed back in our direction! Maybe Dad was trapped and could not get back to us! My mind spun in circles.

I did not know what to do. Dad, our decision-maker, was gone again. Should I bang on the girls' door and get Ruth to drive us out of here? I paced in front of the window.

Then, I saw car lights moving down the road. Dad turned into the driveway and stopped beside the front door. I met him at the bottom of the stairs.

"Is the fire coming back? Do we have to leave?" I asked with more concern than I had intended.

Ruth poked her head around the corner. "What's going on?"

"It's okay," Dad reassured us. "Come on up and I'll tell you."

I do not know where Mishal was at that point. Maybe she was playing with Ruth's things or adrift at sea in the bathtub. I just know she was not part of the conversation.

Dad told us what he had learned.

"I drove down to Jacksons'. Fire crews are setting up down there. The wind has switched and is now out of the west. The fire jumped back across the road and into those trees. It's headed toward Jackson's fields and the creek bottom…"

I interrupted. "Do we have to leave?"

"No, they think we will be okay here. They are bringing in heavy equipment to set up firebreaks."

I thought of the wall of flame Dad and I had flown over a few hours ago. I doubted that even a giant CAT could stop that much fire. Dad continued to talk while I was thinking about this.

"…be a fireline setup down around the corner by those gravel pits. Mark, I will drop you off down there in the morning."

He meant the gravel pits a half mile farther down Gas Well, not the ones I played in all summer.

"You kids get ready for bed. It could be a long day tomorrow."

I tried not to look out the window again; instead, I plodded down the steps to my room. Forget the bath. I was going to man a fireline tomorrow, whatever that was.

The next morning, I dressed in my normal homestead clothes of lace-up leather boots, jeans, a flannel shirt, and a light jacket, with a pair of cotton gloves shoved in one pocket. The sun was up, and I did not think I needed anything more. Besides, I was headed for a fireline. Dad chose a shovel from the woodshed, popped open the trunk lid of the Impala, and placed the shovel inside.

"Let's go," he said, banging the trunk closed.

I slid into the front seat across from him and we turned onto Gas Well Road, there were no columns of smoke like there had been the previous day. We continued around the corner and headed south for a half mile. Pale fingers of smoke drifted across the road a distance away. Dad slowed the car. A couple hundred yards ahead was a line of parked cars and trucks with a knot of people nearby. Beyond the vehicles, a CAT (what Alaskans call any heavy equipment that runs on a track) lumbered out of the ditch, crossed the road, and proceeded toward the smoke. Dad parked and we got out. He opened the trunk, handed me the shovel, and we crunched across the gravel to where the people were gathered, including boys not much older than me. Everyone focused on a man, a man I didn't recognize. His authoritative voice carried across the crowd.

A CAT Making a Fireline

"We have three CATs working the north side of the fire and two on the west side...over there." He pointed to where we had seen the CAT cross the road. Then he turned, faced the left side of the road, and continued.

"We need some men to work the hot spots on the east side of the road.

You can see the smoke. We have a few water packs for those who know how to use one."

Turning to the youth, he instructed, "You kids, go to the west side and look for smoke. It's mostly burned out but there may be a few hot spots yet. Any questions?"

Dad motioned me to join the other boys already moving to the west. "I'll check back around noon," he told me.

With that, he drove off. I could follow directions, work hard, and I could always walk home if I had to. It was only a half mile.

I grabbed my shovel behind the blade and hurried to catch up with the other boys. I knew better than to run with my shovel over my shoulder. I had seen Dad walking with a shovel over his shoulder one day and tried to mimic him. I was fine until I straggled behind and ran to catch up. The bouncing shovel quickly left bruises on my shoulder.

I caught up with the other boys and realized they were older than me. They seemed to know one another, too. I did not recognize any of them. I was not intimidated yet needed more information.

"Uh, hi."

They turned and saw me.

They did not seem unfriendly, though they glanced at my shovel. Maybe they thought I needed a shorter one.

"What are we supposed to do?" I asked. Oh, dumb question, as though I hadn't listened to the man's instructions.

The boys laughed. "Just follow us. We'll show you."

Thus encouraged, I trailed along, not in the actual group, but a bit behind. Soon, we were walking through a thin stand of burned, stunted back spruce. The soil here must have been poor, or the water table too shallow. Whatever the reason, the 10-to-15-foot trees looked like burnt cotton swabs, with a tight cluster of short branches on top and skinny, branchless trunks below. The burnt moss was in knee-high clumps and hard underfoot, too, not as soft and cushiony as I expected. The uneven terrain made walking difficult, and I soon lagged behind the rest.

"There's some smoke!" I heard the cry go up ahead of me and saw the boys running.

I did not see any smoke and didn't hurry.

To my right, I heard the snort of a diesel engine and the rattle of metal tracks. Through the burned trees, I could see a CAT and went to investigate. Perhaps it was attempting to make the firebreak the boys had described. I watched it struggle. It pushed forward a little; then, the tracks spun. It backed up and tried again. The pitiful progress was absurd. These were tiny trees, and the enormous CAT could not push them over. When Dad had our airstrip cleared, I had watched a CAT knock over large stumps without stopping. At this rate, pushing the firebreak a half mile would take weeks.

Eventually, the sluggish equipment moved on, and being curious, I walked over to examine the situation. I nearly fell flat on my back when I stepped onto the break. The scraped ground was still frozen solid, although the vegetation had been dry. No wonder the CAT had been spinning. The tracks could not gain traction on the ice! I moved off the glazed ground and continued parallel to the break. The entire section was frozen. I turned and headed back through the burned trees, my boots kicking up clouds of powdery ash. Here and there, I found a little tendril of smoke and used my shovel to extinguish it down to the final spark. I now knew why the ground was so hard underfoot. Even though the fire had burned intensely, the ground below the moss was still ice-covered. Where there had been flames, there was also ice. Fire and ice. I meandered in the general direction of the parked cars and was soon back in the open.

Someone had set up tables on a gravel pad close to the cars. Behind one table, women were handing out sandwiches and pop. I walked over, waited my turn, and accepted the offerings, then looked for a place to sit.

No chairs. I found a spot away from the foot traffic, set down my shovel, and parked myself next to it. One of the boys came over.

"I see you found your way back," he said.

"I just looked for the cars."

"And the food, too. Huh?" he teased.

I laughed.

Dad showed up after I had finished lunch, and we drove back to the homestead. On the way he gave me the good news.

"It looks like the fire is under control."

I hoped it would not flare up again. Although I did not think I had done much, I was ready to hang up my shovel. And maybe take a bath to get rid of the smell of smoke.

The fire was indeed under control. The mop-up operation I had witnessed wound down. A crew loaded the equipment on trucks and jiggled down Gas Well Road in search of other work. By the following day, all that remained were charred trees, some standing, some fallen. The world seemed to have forgotten already. But I would never forget.

To this day, when summers become dry, and I smell fire, I search the trees, look for smoke, and feel the dread return.

The summer of 1969 was an exceptionally dry one. According to the Bureau of Land Management (BLM), it was the driest spring on record and set the stage for fires. Bans were in place across the state, yet fires, both man-made and naturally occurring, sprang up anyway. The Echo Lake burn was one of the early fires but just one of many on the Kenai Peninsula. The most extensive fire on the Kenai Peninsula was the Swanson River burn. It was reported on August 2 and raged uncontrolled for most of the month, threatening the cities of Kenai, Soldotna, and Nikiski.

In a typical summer, rains started in late July and intensified in August. This pattern curtailed fire activity. In 1969, the August rains did not come, and temperatures remained above normal, with many daytime temperatures between 75 and 80 degrees. Strong and shifting winds intensified the fire danger. Just as I had witnessed on our flyby of the Echo Lake fire, burning embers carried aloft, started fires ahead of the main wall of fire. In this case, they were carried up to a mile-and-a-half ahead.

When the wind blew from the north, burned spruce needles rained down on our homestead cars even though they were ten miles away from the Swanson River burn.

One week into the event, Bob Seemel, assistant refuge manager for the Kenai National Moose Range was quoted in the *Cheechako News* as saying, "When fires like this get running, only God can put them out." Over 800 firefighters manned the blaze, including fire-jumpers from the Lower 48 states. By the time the rains finally arrived at the end of August, the Swanson River burn had consumed 80,000 acres and was the most expensive fire in the US.

Sources: www.cbc.ca. www.insurancejournal.com

CHAPTER 9
A SIMPLE FATHER-SON GETAWAY

NUMEROUS ACTIVE VOLCANOES dot the Aleutian Range. Of the four across Cook Inlet and immediately to the west of the Kenai Peninsula, Mount Augustine is the only volcanic island. Even though it is active, eruptions are telegraphed in advance by the readings of numerous seismic sensors impaled on its flanks. As such, Dad and I never felt apprehensive when setting out to go beaching-combing on its broad, sandy beaches.

This particular trip was in the late summer of 1970 when I was 14 and Dad wanted to go beachcombing and exploring on Augustine Island. At 280 miles round trip, the island was at the edge of the flying range for the 90-hp J-3. The nose tank held 12 gallons, and the auxiliary wing tanks held another six. This capacity allowed no reserve for miscalculations, detours, or weather delays. Thus, as was customary on trips like this, a five-gallon can of gas was set directly behind the rear seat, ahead of the emergency gear, tie-down ropes, and a funnel that smelled of gasoline from previous refueling episodes.

Around 9 a.m., Dad completed the walk-around preflight. Our departure time had been set by the tide table so we would arrive at our destination close to low tide when the beach would be exposed. By now, I was familiar with the preflight routine. Not only had I dogged Dad's footsteps for years, but from time to time, he had allowed me to be at the controls. I had recently received my first official flight instruction and was eager for more. Since the airplane had been built with dual controls, front and back, I placed my hand on the throttle when he reached in to switch on the ignition. Slouching slightly to extend the reach of my still-short legs, I positioned my boot heels on the right and left brakes.

Dad walked around to the front of the plane and placed his hands on the prop.

"Clear!" he called out, letting me know he was about to pull the prop through.

"Clear!" I echoed, confirming I was ready.

The first time, nothing happened. With the second pull, the engine gave a pop and then started. While Dad walked around the prop and then swung himself up into the front seat, I kept my hand firmly on the throttle, ready to give it a slight bump forward if the engine sputtered. My job ended when Dad was aboard, placed his hand on the throttle, and I was once again just a passenger in the back seat.

We proceeded down the taxiway, turned left, and headed to the south end of the homestead runway. Dad completed the simple pre-takeoff checklist, advanced the throttle, and after bouncing briefly down the grassy turf we were airborne.

I assumed Dad had checked the weather. My first impression of the day's condition was when we began our ascent to 5,000 feet, an altitude required for the J-3 to glide safely to shore in the event of engine failure over Cook Inlet. Pilots had a healthy respect for the frigid, unforgiving waters of the Inlet. Those who tempted fate seldom got a second chance.

From this lofty perch, I scanned the clouds and terrain to the west and south, which was the direction we were headed. As a rule, storms moved in from that direction, which meant if the weather took a turn for the worse, we would be running away from it on our flight back home. Today, clouds lay draped across the entire area in scattered bands, from 11,000 feet down to 6,000 feet. The tallest volcanoes poked their heads through lower layers, leaving a skirt of gray around their midriffs. The lower reaches were cloud-free, which was a good sign. Above the mountain crowns, a solid layer of overcast prevented sunshine from brightening the day any further. An experienced pilot would consider these observations, continue to monitor them, and proceed accordingly.

Still, it was not a bad day for flying. Visibility was quite good, and to the north, I could see as far as Mount McKinley, more than 150 miles away. This distance is not uncommon in Alaska, whereas pilots visiting from Outside are accustomed to vistas frequently obscured by dust, humidity, or air pollution and are astonished by the clarity. To the south, the dark clouds hinted at possible precipitation. We could not actually see Mount Augustine, although that did not necessarily imply anything ominous. It was still 100 miles away and hidden beyond the curvature of the earth.

We completed the crossing and turned southward. Now that we were safely back over land, Dad eased back on the throttle and let the nose down to scrub some altitude. Spotting moose, swans, or other wildlife was easier from 1,000 feet than 5,000. Besides, the coast here had numerous beaches suitable for an emergency landing if required. At the foot of the tall mountains on our right, rivers and streams filled with snowmelt broke up the landscape of swamps and groves of spruce trees.

Over the years, I had flown this route many times with Dad, and I knew where the cabins, set-net sites, and duck-hunting shacks were located. I also learned about prominent landmarks. After crossing a low peninsula called Harriet Point, Dad began to climb to 3,000 feet to cross Tuxedni Bay. At the mouth of the Bay was Chisik Island, a mile-and-a-half wedge of rock, with the low point facing east into Cook Inlet and the buttress ending toward the headwaters and mountains.

We skimmed over the top of the south side of the island and across a narrow channel where a cannery stood on stilts at the water's edge. Here the local commercial set-net fisherman sold their catch. That seasonal dot of civilization soon passed behind us. Again, we dipped lower to follow the beach past Johnson River, Silver Salmon Creek, and toward Chinitna Bay.

Dad banked the airplane slightly and pointed to a grizzly with a pair of this year's cubs strolling on the beach ahead. Disturbed by the sound of the J-3, they hustled through the tall grass that bordered the beach and into the short, thick spruce beyond. These were not the only bears around. Bear tracks appeared everywhere, especially along the banks of the small freshwater streams, which provided spawning grounds for salmon. Bear country was not a place we would intentionally spend the night outdoors unless within the secure walls of a cabin or other well-built structure.

We approached Chinitna Bay and Dad throttled up as we headed to 4,500 feet to cross the bay and on to Augustine. For 20 miles or so, the country south of Chinitna Bay offered little in the way of landing spots, and as a prudent pilot, he was taking preventive measures. Instead of pleasant sandy crescents, the shoreline consisted of jagged outcroppings, plummeting from 5,000-foot peaks to the crashing surf below. We avoided this area and cut through a low pass on the inland side.

Dad's head and shoulders obstructed my view, and I scooted left and right to peer around him as best I could. Finally, I saw the shoreline of Augustine. Where was the peak we had seen before? The summit was only 4,000 feet tall. The cloud deck must have decreased. Not only that, but intermittent drops of rain also started to pelt against the windshield and an occasional rivulet snaked its way past my side window. Now and then, an occasional jolt of turbulence penetrated the din of the engine. The weather was deteriorating.

Dad was now flying parallel to Augustine, hugging the coast instead of heading across the water toward the island. He kept looking back and forth between the weather ahead and the island, 12 miles to our left. Below us, I saw wind streaking out of the channels and whitecaps on the ocean. There was tremendous wind down there, and it was from the north. My heart beat faster. I was no longer enjoying sightseeing from the back seat. I silently willed Dad to turn around, but he didn't.

Dad twisted slightly in the front seat and yelled back at me. "The ceiling's too low to cross here. Let's try the next point!"

My nod lacked enthusiasm.

The next point of land, about six to seven miles south, was closer to Mount Augustine and could be crossed safely at a lower altitude. I recognized Dad's intent to salvage the trip by crossing there. But there was a problem. A big one. The farther south we flew, the lower the cloud ceiling dropped. After reaching the second point and seeing that a safe crossing was not possible, Dad banked the J-3 and we headed back the way we had just come.

Dad descended to 3,000 feet to stay under the clouds as we headed south. Now, he climbed back up to clear the mountains. The little airplane was willing to claw back the altitude, but we were not making much progress northward. In fact, we seemed to be barely creeping forward at all. The rain became heavier, and the ragged clouds rushed by, dragging their wet fingers along the rock-strewn mountains on either side of us.

I knew my dad had hours of treacherous flying under his belt and had always finagled his way out of bad situations; all the same, my nervousness increased. In the brief time I had spent at the controls of the J-3, I had already learned I was more comfortable in the front seat at the controls than in the back seat as a passenger. I mentally began to question what was going on in front of me. *Does Dad see how slow we are going? Why is he flying so close to those rocks? I think we need more altitude.* My mind raced as it processed different scenarios, none of them good. In uneven spurts, I sucked in my breath. The harsh turbulence continued non-stop and at times, yanked me hard against my seatbelt. We still had not made much progress northward.

Again, Dad turned partway around and yelled, "We need to clear this saddle between the ridges and then it will smooth out."

I wondered if he said that for my sake or his. For one second, I pondered what he had said, and then a gust of wind, boiling over the top of the ridge, grabbed the light airplane and pitched it completely over on its side. With horror, I stared straight at the ground. I grabbed the cross-bracing above my head. The airplane continued to roll, and the nose rotated until it pointed straight down. Then weightlessness. Time froze. Dirt slowly rose from the floorboards. I watched a candy bar from the baggage compartment drift by in slow motion. Hershey's. Plain. I was going to die, splattered on the mountainside, like the wrecked airplanes I had seen in mountain passes.

Then, with a bang, the tiny, fabric-clothed aircraft valiantly flew through the spiraling maelstrom, and weight returned. We sagged in our seats as Dad regained control and pulled the nose up sharply.

Abandoning the attempt to head farther north, Dad again pointed the J-3 southward. Back over the rugged shoreline, he searched for a place to set down and wait out the storm. There were no sandy areas of any length. The only viable landing area was at the most 400 to 500 feet long, barely long enough. Beyond that stretch, there were airplane-wrecking boulders. And the approach was over a 30-foot cliff. To the north, the jagged cliff grew to over 1,000 feet. Though we were somewhat protected by the cliffs and not experiencing the full force of the wind, streaks on the water were a vivid reminder of the intensity of the storm. I knew, and I was sure Dad did, too, that turbulence, or a severe downdraft by the cliffs, was a distinct possibility.

The Beach Where Elmer Landed the J-3

My heart raced as we descended toward the landing site. I gripped the bracing overhead with white knuckles. As Dad guided it lower and lower, the airplane danced but remained controllable. Then, in sharp contrast to the previous 15 minutes, we touched down lightly on the smooth sand and quickly came to a halt. I fully understood some people's inclination to get out and kiss the ground. I wanted to hug that bit of an airplane, too, which had once again gotten us safely back to earth.

I could not see Dad's face. I wondered what my unshakable father was feeling. Without a word, he switched off the engine, and we sat for a moment, the airplane rocking slightly in the gusts. All was quiet except for the whistle of the wind and the ping of the cooling exhaust.

"I figured we had only one shot at landing here," he remarked. "The wind was just so squirrelly."

"No kidding!" I replied, perhaps more sullenly than I should have. My emotions were in turmoil, not unlike the wildly churning wind we had just flown through. On the one hand, I was relieved to have survived and once again be on solid ground; on the other hand, I was angry at having been put in a life-threatening condition to begin with.

Mark standing beside the J-3

Dad summed up the situation.

"We are going to be here for a while, so let's tie down the airplane, gas it up, and go exploring."

With that, he opened the clam-shell door and climbed out—the practical optimist. I clambered out and joined him in front of the airplane.

Since the airplane was our only ticket out of this mess, keeping it safe was a top priority. Cook Inlet's large tides are always a consideration along the coast, and being aware of the tidal patterns is essential for private pilots and boat captains alike. The reach of the previous high tide was scribed as a thin line of kelp and other small bits of flotsam on the beach. Easy to read, yet we did not have a lot of leeway to play with. This under-sized piece of beach backed against a cliff, with the foot of it lined in a tangle of driftwood.

"The tide will be up here in a couple of hours," Dad said, looking out at the water and then back at the plane.

We exchanged a few words and agreed. I figured if we pulled the tail of the J-3 as far up as possible toward the cliff, the main gear would stay clear of the water.

Securing the airplane was no problem with the plentiful driftwood. We worked without advising each other what needed to be done. Dad tilted the rear seat up, pulled out ropes, and handed me one. I walked around to the far side, fastened one end around a log, and knotted the other around the tie-down point on the wing. With the airplane secure, I reached into the baggage compartment and pulled out the funnel with the attached chamois-skin filter. Dad was already standing on the tire to reach the nose tank and remove the gas cap.

"Here, Dad." I handed him the funnel.

He locked it in place and balanced with one foot on the tire and the other on the gear-leg step. I uncapped the gas can and lifted it within his reach. He expertly tipped it onto the funnel, and gasoline gurgled into the nose tank.

After refueling was completed, we walked the beach to get an idea of what we would have available for takeoff once the tide receded.

On the short hike back to the J-3, Dad outlined a plan to use up several hours as we waited for the tide to turn.

"I saw some interesting rock formations on our approach to this spot," he said, as if trying to navigate the airplane down and save our lives had not consumed every ounce of his focus.

"You mean that bluish-greenish band on the side of the cliff back there?" I asked. I, too, had seen the formation, right before I got a death grip on the overhead braces.

"Right. Maybe we can find some smaller pieces to take back as samples," Dad suggested. "Oh, and let's grab our fishing poles while we are at it."

"Okay," I responded. What else could I say?

Dad's fascination with rocks was something he had developed later in life. I am not sure when it happened, but out of the blue he went from banning three-pound hiking boots as a luxury item in the airplane to deciding a 50-pound rock was a high priority.

Mark in His Mom-Made Rain Gear

The rain had let up briefly when we had landed but had started up again. I donned the makeshift rain gear Mom had stitched together out of Visqueen. While it kept the rain off, I knew from experience if I hiked for long, condensation would dampen me from the inside out. We grabbed the fishing poles, a small plastic tackle box, and a packboard. We could not walk the beach back toward the blue-green formation since the cliff we had flown over to land blocked our path. We would have to climb the grassy notch behind the airplane.

When we reached the top, the wind once again raged against us. The wind gusts had knocked the moisture off the grass and low shrubs. Our cotton gloves remained dry, and the climb up the cliff warmed us inside our medium-weight jackets. This far south, on the west side of Cook Inlet, there were few trees, and the terrain was primarily tundra, with patches of willows; although some gullies were choked with leg-grabbing alders.

After we had walked along the top of the cliff for about a half mile, we arrived at a small lake we had seen from the air. Amidst a flying nightmare, Dad remembered even this specific location. That was why Dad had suggested we hike up with fishing poles. He always had a backup plan.

"Let's try here," Dad said, stopping in his tracks. He spoke casually as if we had not just escaped death in the airplane and were merely on a father-son afternoon fishing outing.

"Okay. Maybe a small spinner?" I suggested.

"That should work."

I noticed the lake was relatively shallow, and the stream at the outlet plunged 30 feet onto the beach below. Could a salmon climb that waterfall, even at a very high tide? I doubted it.

"What are we fishing for?"

With a wry smile, Dad turned to me and said, "Whatever is in there."

Fortunately, the wind was at our backs, so even though our hiking boots kept us confined to the lake bank's dryness, we were able to send our fishing lures zinging well out into the lake. I didn't think a single fish had ever swum in those waters. We were just killing time.

After thrashing the water unsuccessfully, we stowed the lures in the tackle box and hiked back to the cliff edge to search for a way down to the beach and look for the intriguing rock formation. Ten minutes later, we found another grassy chute and half-slid half-ran the 30 feet to the bottom. We shuffled through the sand in the direction we had seen the formation and wove around large water-smoothed boulders at the base of the cliff.

Sure enough, a vein of blue-green rock about 20 feet wide ran out of the ocean and diagonally up the cliff at a shallow angle. Some pieces of the formation lay in the sand; however, the smallest was the size of a serving platter, larger than we wanted to pack back to the airplane.

"I'll see if I can break one of these pieces up," I told Dad.

He had already found another chunk to work on.

I picked up a piece and dashed it against a boulder. A few shards flew in all directions. I lifted the rock and tried again. Before long, we had a half-dozen egg-sized pieces. Dad's half-smile registered his satisfaction. We pocketed our treasures, climbed back up the grassy draw, and made our way back along the cliff edge in the direction of the J-3.

From our vantage point, the airplane appeared to be in an impossible spot for takeoff. No useable beach remained, and the waves surged within a few feet of the tires. The J-3 seemed pinned against the rocks, like a caribou backed into a corner by ravenous wolves. Nevertheless, the tide book said the waters should retreat shortly and that retreat would resurrect our beach. We just had to be patient.

Back down at the airplane, we dug out our lunches and refueled ourselves. The peanut butter sandwiches Mom had packed for us hit the spot. We usually did not carry water on our trips since we drank stream water or snowmelt. In this case, however, Dad had packed a flask of water since we had intended to spend the day on Augustine Island, where fresh water could be difficult to find. What we would not drink we would pour out before our flight continued. No use carrying unnecessary weight when we had picked up rocks.

The tidewater began to recede and let go of the airplane tires. I wandered along the skimpy shoreline as our fragment of an airstrip reemerged. I caught sight of white-winged gulls and other coastal birds circling. They survived, even thrived, in this environment. I couldn't help but smile.

Focusing again on the sandy beach, I poked at the debris that had washed up with the latest tide. More kelp, bits of driftwood, and a few beaten mollusk shells. Items from nature. Nothing that reflected human contact. Through my experiences on the Kenai Peninsula, including its coasts, I learned ocean currents carried different materials to different seashores. The currents around Augustine Island made it a trap for all kinds of flotsam and jetsam. This stretch of shoreline was litter-free.

As the tide changed, the wind lost some of its ferocity, although the plane rocked slightly as we sat inside waiting for the tide's continued retreat. Regardless of the diminished wind, I did not necessarily want to get back in the air. It could be said, literally, that we were between a rock and a hard place.

Finally, Dad reckoned the beach sufficiently clear.

"Let's get moving," he said, swinging his legs over the side of the airplane door.

"I'll untie the tail," I volunteered.

Dad removed the ropes from the wings, and I tossed them into the baggage compartment.

Dad was itching to go. He paced around the plane, performing a quick preflight. Together, we pushed the J-3 from its snug refuge and pointed it down the beach. Once more, I swung myself into the back seat and snugged my seatbelt. Really snug! While Dad hand-propped the engine, I kept my hand on the throttle and brakes. With the engine running, Dad got aboard, looked over the control panel, and outside the plane windows. Now that we were getting ready to take off again, my stomach tightened, and the anxiety returned. We were about to fly over the same terrain that had beat us up just a few hours before. Were we going to have to go through that again? I sure hoped not!

Dad advanced the throttle and within 100 feet we were airborne. He banked the plane away from the cliff and over to the open water, where he circled to gain altitude.

I immediately assessed the weather. The cloud ceiling was higher than when we had been forced down. No rain. Still a stiff wind, but our progress northward seemed slightly faster, although most pilots regard the terms "J-3" and "faster" as mutually exclusive. Still, it was an improvement. The saddle in the mountains that had nearly swatted us out of the sky was coming toward us. I held my breath and gripped the crossbars. This time, Dad was able to fly higher and gain some space between us and the top of the saddle. The terrain turbulence still jostled us, but nothing nearly as cruel as what we had experienced in that spot previously. I released my grip on the crossbars and let my shoulders droop in relief.

Although the wind had subsided to some degree, progress was pitifully slow, and if airplanes could trudge, that was what we were doing on our return. We were still 120 miles from home and doubtfully making 60 mph against the wind. At least we were now over familiar territory, and beaches were plentiful for emergency landings. That was the good news.

But I had been watching Dad. He kept fiddling with something under the dash and then looking at the gas indicator in the nose tank, just beyond the windshield. I knew what he was checking. The wing tank used gravity to drain fuel into the nose tank, which then supplied fuel for the engine. He was checking to see if all the fuel from the wing had drained into the nose tank. I could see the indicator bouncing up and down ahead of the windshield. It read about three-fourths full and had not gone up, as would be expected when the wing tank replenished the nose tank. Dad had been checking to make sure the wing tank had drained completely, and it had.

That meant we did not have the fuel necessary to get home. The extra flying time to the south and then back against a strong headwind had burned through far more fuel than he had anticipated. Bad news. At least we were over friendly territory, except for the grizzlies promenading on the beaches. More bad news. Yet, there was still daylight. Good news.

As we neared Silver Salmon Creek, Dad circled one of the set-net sites and made his approach to land on the beach. I knew this fish site. It was owned by the Denman's. I had fished for salmon behind their cabin. It was just south of the fish sites owned by the Kruger's and Bell's, who had already packed up for the season. Dad touched down on the perfectly smooth beach and rolled to a stop in front of the cabin.

The J-3 Parked on the Beach by the Denman's Cabin

Tom Denman, dressed in dark coveralls, a blue hat, and knee-high black rubber boots, came out to greet us. Undoubtedly, he wanted to get the latest news and see what caused the unexpected visit. While the adults exchanged pleasantries, I ambled up the beach looking for seashells, all the while keeping an eye out for bears. When I returned, Dad had bought enough gas from this helpful fisherman to get us home. With the nose tank topped off, we were soon airborne.

I watched the familiar Alaskan wilderness scroll by beneath me. No roads or cabins marked this country, but I knew the creeks, hills, and beaches almost as well as I knew our homestead. Dull streaks of gray filled the sky. Still, as with the barren cliffside, there was beauty and life in the wildness. Numerous small rivers, some clear, some green with glacial silt, wove their serpentine paths through the hills and valleys. An occasional moose appeared in a swamp and every now and then a pair of swans stood out in sharp contrast to dark pond water. To my left, the ice-cold, glacier-covered flanks of Mount Redoubt played hide-and-seek in the clouds. Whether in the woods, on a beach, or here in the sky, this frontier was my home.

The flight back to the homestead was ending safely, yet I had to admit there really was no simple father-son flying experience with my dad. It was becoming apparent that he and I had different degrees of risk tolerance, and sometimes, I wished I was at the controls.

Dad took the turquoise rocks in to be assayed, and they proved to be low-grade copper ore.

CHAPTER 10
OVER THE EDGE

I WATCHED ANXIOUSLY as my classmates grew by leaps and bounds while I seemed mired in silty beach mud. I was not the first pick for sports. For class pictures, I always found myself in the front row. Yet, as much as my failure to grow was annoying, it did not curtail my hunting and flying. I already had five years of hunting experience under my belt, including several in the mountains above timberline. These accomplishments bolstered my sense of identity and even drew respect from some of the bigger guys.

All my hunts had been with Dad and my experiences had led me to conclude that he and I did not process information in the same way. That is, he believed there was always a way up or down a mountain, the weather would improve, and a ring of bologna and a loaf of bread would stave off starvation. I, on the other hand, saw the possibility of getting trapped above a cliff, sunshine instantly turning to rain, and my rifle jamming while a grizzly chased me.

We differed in other ways, too. Whereas I jumped at the chance to improve our hunting well-being by expanding our menu with innovative granola bars and pre-packaged meals, Dad never wavered from bologna and chocolate bars. And I heard rumors of hunting gear upgrades, such as camp stoves and compact foam mats. But none of these advancements entered conversations with Dad. He wanted the tried and true.

I also knew that when hunting with my confident father, I would likely experience moments of panic. Regardless, when he talked about another goat hunt, any misgiving evaporated like a morning mist.

Because Dad and his partner, Dr. Paul Isaak, patched up oilfield worker accidents and delivered babies around the clock, he rationed his time carefully. Subsequently, my hunts with Dad were typically single-day events. This hunt would be different. Regulations had changed. Now, hunters could not hunt the same day they were airborne. That meant we would be out for at least two days. Dad's plan for this hunt was to take our game by noon on the second day and fly back before nightfall.

On that Friday afternoon in early September, the sun smiled everywhere. Dad and I gathered our hunting gear and drove to Sports Lake, where he tied down the J-3 on floats for the summer.

He had been at the office that day but left a few hours early so we could fly into the Kenai Mountains, 40 miles to the east, and set up camp before dark. When we arrived at the lake, I helped him load the plane. As always, we were wearing hip boots when we flew a plane on floats.

"Hand me the sleeping bags," Dad said.

"Here you go. Tent next?" I responded.

"Yes."

We had developed an unspoken way of loading the plane and by habit we worked together. I was no longer a kid waiting to be told what to do. The 8mm rifle would follow the tent with the lightweight frame packboards on top. Dad tucked small bags with extra clothes and food into the remaining crannies and corners. I untied the wings.

Dad hopped onto a float. I remained on the shore, holding the aircraft's tail while he made a quick pre-flight inspection and walked to the front of the float to start the engine.

He turned to me. "You ready?"

"Yep," I replied.

He propped the engine to life. After he had climbed into the front seat, I sprang onto a float and pulled myself into the back seat.

We were soon airborne and flying at a brisk 80 mph. As we headed east, Dad kept the plane low over the trees and swamps to look for game. Twenty minutes later, he throttled up to gain altitude over the mountains. The lake, where we were going to set up camp, was in a narrow valley perpendicular to the east side of Skilak Glacier, one of the many glacial fingers extending from the massive Harding Icefield. The lake was at 3,000 feet, well above the treeline, which made it an ideal base camp for alpine hunting. At that elevation, the few willow bushes made for an easy hike. Visibility was restricted only by the terrain.

Before landing, Dad circled, and we scanned the mountainsides for mountain goats in the immediate region. From experience, we knew they moved around considerably but favored this area. Sure enough, in no time, we picked out white dots on the mountainside about a mile away. Dad banked the plane back toward the lake to keep from disturbing these keen-eyed critters and prepared to land.

While this sliver of water was almost a mile long, at its narrowest point it was under 100 feet wide. Landing was a bit like threading a needle. Sharp, float-piercing rocks bordered most of the lake's shoreline, with only a few narrow strips of sand to safely beach the aircraft. Dad touched down on the lake and taxied toward one of those bands, located at the east end of the lake where a stream drained into the Skilak Glacier Canyon.

He shut off the engine as we drew close, and we gently coasted toward shore. As we drifted, I watched the rocks on the bottom and remembered that crystal-clear water creates an illusion of size and depth. On a previous occasion, I had stepped off the floats, believing the water was knee-deep, and found it pouring over the tops of my hip boots. That was a mistake not to be repeated.

After tying the plane securely to some willows along the shore, we unloaded and searched for a campsite for our tent.

What about here?" I asked.

"Not too bad…looks a little damp, though. Let's look around a little more."

Nothing was flat. Some areas were just *less steep* than others. Too often, I had fought with a slippery sleeping bag sliding in the tent. How annoying for it, and everything else, to gravitate toward the downhill end of the tent. Fortunately, on this hunt, we found a reasonably level spot. By the time we had set up the small two-man tent and stowed our gear, it was nearly dark. Before settling in, Dad strolled to the lakeshore to confirm the plane was secure, and then once back inside the tent, we zipped close the tent flap.

Well, we will want to get an early start." Dad always said that. "You ready?" He was talking about lights out, not the hunt. I removed my glasses and tucked them in a tent pocket by my elbow.

"I am now," I replied.

And with that, he switched off the flashlight.

I lay in the dark, listening. In the distance, I heard the faint rush of a waterfall, and I smiled. I loved it up here.

When the sky brightened the next morning, we awoke to clear, frosty air. After a brief breakfast of Mom's homemade cinnamon rolls, washed down with slurps of cold lake water, we prepared to climb the mountain.

Our packs were light and contained only the bare necessities for the day: the 8mm Mauser rifle with a box of 20 shells, three hunting knives, three game bags, two bologna sandwiches, two candy bars, extra gloves, the ever-present but never used compass, basic first-aid kit, waterproof matches, and a space blanket. We distributed these items into two of the game bags, and, with many feet of clothesline, secured these to our aluminum-frame packboards.

Before leaving the lake, we had to ford a small stream at its outlet. It was only 20 feet or so across and no more than knee-deep. Not a big deal. We had brought hiking boots for the hunt but wore our hip boots to cross the stream. Once across, we changed and left the hip boots on the stream bank.

We crisscrossed upward and westward with Dad in the lead and the sun warming our backs. Snowpack remained in many draws and ravines since the previous winter had been unusually snowy, and we had had a cooler-than-normal summer. For the moment, it meant plenty of water to refresh ourselves as we ascended. Later in the day, the snow would become a problem.

Soon the mild weather and our exertion forced us to remove our jackets, and we roped them to our packs. Climbing steadily, we made good headways, and we topped the ridge well before noon. It was the kind of day when it seemed nothing could go wrong. It would be a quick hunt, and I would be back in my bed that night.

"We should probably check the northeastern side first, then work our way westward," suggested Dad. "That way, if we spook the goats, we will be above them, and they will run out of cover to hide to the west."

"Sounds good to me," I responded.

Even though we did not seriously want to find goats in that area, we cautiously hiked off the summit to inspect the rugged cliffs below. Retrieving a downed animal in that terrain would mean rappelling, something for which we had neither the equipment nor the desire to do. Nonetheless, we needed to be thorough and check to see if goats were in that area. Since they moved around, it was possible they would move to terrain where we could take a shot. Discovering nothing, we climbed back to the top and headed westward.

I always found hunting on top of a mountain exhilarating. The walking was easy; panoramic views stretched to the horizon, and there was the anticipation that our prize lay beyond the next rise or dip.

We stopped for lunch at the western end of the ridge and positioned ourselves to survey the rocky terrain below and to the sides. A light breeze played across our faces, and high clouds that had drifted across the sun stole some of the warmth. All the same, we were comfortable.

I could not get enough of the spectacular views. Skilak Glacier lay at our feet, some 3,500 feet below. About three miles to our right, and at our elevation, the white expanse of the Harding Icefield stretched southward; the 6,000-foot-thick ice field was from an Ice Age in North America.

After we finished our sandwiches, we shouldered our packs and stealthily inched our way down the western end of the mountain. A short time later, we paused and scanned the country below for the elusive goats. After a couple of minutes, out of the corner of his eye, Dad spotted movement. He nudged me and pointed. Sure enough, a herd of four or five young billies grazed in a grass-filled pocket about 300 yards below us.

"They are in a pretty good spot," I whispered.

Dad nodded and indicated a narrow trail meandering between rocky outcrops below us.

"It's a pretty long shot from here," he replied softly. "Let's see if we can work our way down without spooking them."

"Sure," I replied.

Hidden from view by the rock formations, we carefully picked our way toward our next viewing post. Through example and an occasional stern look, Dad had taught me how to tread silently on various types of ground, which took multitasking to a new level. We had to keep an eye on the ground for loose rocks that might rattle downslope and alert the game, search for handholds, and watch for our quarry. With enough experience, this simultaneous attention became second nature.

We reached our chosen spot and found the goats still feeding, unalarmed. Dad motioned for me to set up for the shot. He moved to one side to keep track of whichever goat I shot. I carefully chambered one of the three-inch long, 155-grain rounds and settled in to take the shot. I was not hunting for a trophy, so I selected the animal that presented the cleanest profile and squeezed off the round. While watching for the goat's reaction, I rapidly chambered a second round. The goats fled and headed for rocky cliffs to the right. The goat I had targeted lagged and stumbled slightly. I acquired him in my riflescope a second time, tracked him briefly, and gently pulled the trigger again. This time, the goat fell and remained still.

"Good shooting," Dad remarked as we worked our way down to the dead animal.

"I don't know why he didn't drop with that first shot. He was a way downhill. Maybe that threw me off." I was a bit miffed my first shot did not down the animal.

Now, the real work began. Dad expertly began to skin the animal, then let me continue to remove the hide from the neck,

"Looks like your first shot got a front quarter," Dad said, pointing to the damaged leg.

I winced inwardly. Dad's comment was not a rebuke, just a statement of the facts. He had taught me to avoid wasting meat by placing my shots in the small area just behind the front shoulder. My slight miscalculation had cost us some meat.

"Yeah. That's unfortunate," I said.

We then de-boned the quarters to minimize the weight we had to pack back to camp. Once we picked the carcass clean, we removed the head and

 I slipped the pack with the abbreviated hide, horns, and hiking gear over my shoulders. Dad shrugged on the pack with the meat. He also carried the rifle. The plan was to traverse the mountainside eastward and descend gradually while staying above the scrubby willow and occasional clumps of mountain ash and alders. Ahead of us, we could see some substantial patches of snow clinging to the steep mountainside. As always, I followed behind Dad.

When we approached the first snowfield, I watched him step onto the edge. We had expected the meager heat of the day to soften the snowpack enough to allow an easy, if somewhat soggy, crossing; instead, his boots sunk in only a couple of inches. I hesitantly traced his steps, leaving a space of 20 feet between us. We moved deliberately. Dad stomped on the snow to deepen the track, then took the next step. Neither of us said a word. I began thinking that climbing back up and around the snowfield, even with a pack, might have been a better idea. But here we were.

About halfway across, as he took another step, Dad's feet abruptly flew out from under him. I gasped in disbelief as he accelerated down the mountainside on the hard-crusted snow. Snow sprayed everywhere as he dug in his heels. Desperately, he rammed the butt of the rifle into the snow. It did nothing to slow his rapid plunge. About 100 yards downslope, the icy snow terminated into a pile of rocks. Dad slammed into the rocks, bounced in the air, and disappeared over a cliff. I stood utterly still, transfixed by what had just occurred.

Dad was gone! I was 14 and alone on a treacherous snowslide. What was I going to do? I visualized Dad's battered body on the glacier thousands of feet below me. I had some time at the controls of the J-3, but could I fly myself home to get help? How was I going to get off this snow? Would I be the next to fall?

My careening thoughts were yanked to a halt when I saw something move on the slope, hundreds of yards below me. There, on another patch of snow, Dad, pack still on his back, slid into view. I stared. I had been holding my breath, but now inhaled sharply when I saw him move. With considerable effort, he got to his feet and looked up where I was standing. He waved slowly, and then, in the distance, I heard him yell faintly, "Don't come down that way!"

Yes. Dad's humor was intact.

Now, I was on a mission. I had to go down and help Dad. With a heightened awareness of the rigid snow's hazards, I methodically stamped out a secure footing for each step forward. After some minutes, I crossed the snowfield. Once more, I gained a foothold on solid rock. I don't recall scrambling rapidly down to his location, but I suspect I was really moving.

At the bottom, I found Dad reordering his pack.

"Some of the meat got beat up and wet on the way down," he said. "There is no reason to pack that out now."

I was speechless at his nonchalance.

I regarded him up and down. No bloody head wound. No dragging appendages. No signs of trauma other than a torn pant leg on his now moisture-soaked trousers. Most importantly, he still had his green army surplus hat. I gazed back up the mountain. Indeed, that must have been a wild ride for him. The cliff Dad had slid over was only 15 to 20 feet tall, and the steep, snowy slope below it had helped break his fall. The terrain then flattened out and allowed for a gradual stop, rather than causing him to plow into more rocks or brush or fall another 1,500 feet to the glacier. Dad's guardian angel probably complained about the overtime he had to put in on this assignment.

This unexpected detour presented new considerations. Dad's long descent had taken him far enough down the mountain that we were now about 1,500 feet below the level of our campsite. We were also at an elevation where alders, with their clothes-grabbing branches, were abundant. That meant the uphill trek of several miles would be slow-going and grueling. In addition to that bad news, dusk was settling in. Without comment, we both knew it would be dark before we arrived at the lake. We accepted these facts. Knowing time was wasting, we settled the packs onto our backs and started out. It was then that I noticed Dad's limp and that he was using the rifle like a walking stick.

Elmer on a Better Day of Hunting in the Mountains

Our progress was slow. An hour later, the light was so poor we could barely see where to place our feet. The chill in the air, which came from the sun's setting, was held at bay only by our exertion; nevertheless, Dad's wet clothes made hypothermia a realistic threat. We dared not pause for long. Even though we both knew the general direction of the lake and that it was impossible to miss, the terrain was filled with little hills and ravines, some with trickling streams and some with steep sides. More than once, we had to backtrack to find an alternate path around an obstacle.

The night enveloped us. No moon shone overhead. I lost track of time. I followed Dad, knowing where he was by sound, rather than by sight. When he rested, I bumped into him.

Finally, he cleared his throat and said, "I think we are really close."

How did he know? I strained my eyes. The darkness yielded no clues. Then I heard the slap of waves on the lakeshore and understood. He was using all his senses. We were back.

We headed toward the welcoming sound and intercepted the stream at the lake's outlet. We had a general idea of where we had stashed the hip boots and felt around until we found them. We removed our hiking boots, tied them to our packs, strapped on our hip boots, crossed the stream, and shambled the short distance to our campsite. To me, that little tent was like a luxury suite in a fancy hotel. Inside, Dad poked around for the flashlight he had stowed and switched it on. After walking in the dark, the subdued yellow circle of light seemed painfully bright.

Dad glanced at his watch and then extended his wrist toward me. It was 11 p.m. We had been walking for five hours. With barely enough energy to slip out of our damp clothes, we exchanged them for dry, insulated underwear, and crawled into our sleeping bags. It was then that I saw the angry, deep purple bruise, the size of a grapefruit, on Dad's right thigh and realized why he had been limping. That observation reinforced in my mind that my dad could do anything, including flying us home the next morning.

I was right.

Mark and Elmer after Mark's Second Goat Hunt

CHAPTER 11

THEY ALL LOOK
THE SAME

MY FATHER WAS A MAGNET for adventures. Sometimes, he had only to get out of bed in the morning to start what could evolve into an epic tale at the supper table. No wonder Mom kept an ear out for the sound of his airplane, stared out the window and wrung her hands when he was 15 minutes late or watched for the shine of his car lights coming up the driveway.

And so it was, one morning in November 1972 when I was 16 that Dad and I started out to go moose hunting. In those days, there were two moose hunting seasons on the Kenai Peninsula: one in September, and a late season that ran the last half of November. We had failed to get a moose in the earlier season, so this was a second chance to fill the freezer. For this late-season hunt, it was legal to fly and hunt on the same day.

A few years before, Dad had added another plane to his fleet, a brown-and-yellow Piper PA-12. It was similar to the J-3; however, this larger model had a wide rear seat that held two passengers. It also had a real electrical system with landing and navigation lights, a basic radio, and more instruments. Furthermore, it also had a more powerful 150 hp Lycoming engine and a starter, and there was no more hand-propping.

The night before Dad had prepped the PA-12. He had fueled it, checked the oil, and verified that the duffle of emergency gear and sleeping bags was on board. Then, in the pre-dawn, he walked the 75 yards between the house and hangar and plugged in the electric heater, which was stuffed inside the engine cowling. He then wrapped the cowling in a custom-insulated engine cover.

At the house, we gathered the rest of our hunting gear and staged it at the front door landing. After that, Dad leaped up the stairs to the kitchen, two steps at a time. I followed in like manner.

As her usual efficient self, Mom had prepared a plate of homemade raisin bread toast, which she had baked in large round cans.

"Ah, my favorite, raisin toast!" I exclaimed. "Thanks, Mom."

What a great way to start the day.

No matter how early we left for a hunt, she could be heard in the kitchen heating water for hot cocoa, pulling out the toaster, setting the table, or making other breakfast-making sounds.

She placed a plate of oleomargarine on the table and paused behind her chair. We bowed our heads, and Dad blessed the food. After the "amen," Dad picked up a box of Cornflakes and shook the open end until an avalanche of dry, golden cereal spilled into his bowl. I did the same. Soon, my cereal was swimming in watery powdered milk.

"I hope we get something," I said, stating the obvious.

Mom continued puttering around the kitchen while paying attention to her husband and son at the table. "Me, too. We are getting low on moose," she acknowledged.

Dad summed it up. "We'll see what we can find."

When we moved to Alaska, Mom easily adapted to the lean, coarse-grained meat, and after serving it numerous times to guests, had earned a reputation for making one of the best moose roasts around; in fact, at some point, she won a cooking contest with her recipe. Not only that, but she often hunted moose with Dad and me, although that was when we hunted by road, in a car, not an airplane.

Knowing Mom, anticipating our successful hunt, she would make space to hang moose quarters in the woodshed before we returned.

Dad swallowed a spoonful of cereal and then added his comments. "I heard several folks got moose to the north of here. The ice on the lakes is plenty thick, too." His daily interaction with the local people, many of them hunters, provided a valuable source of hunting information.

Mom glanced at him, and her brow creased. I knew what she was thinking: *I don't want my menfolk to fall through the ice with the plane.*

Dad was already on his second piece of toast. I hastened my pace. He was out of his chair as I took my last bite. Mom picked up our plates and handed me a packed lunch. When I turned around, Dad had already pulled on his green army coat and was reaching for our gear.

Learning to fly was almost a family tradition. Even Mom had taken some flight instruction, and I had early recollections of riding in the backseat of the airplane while the instructor coaxed Mom through basic flight maneuvers. Now it was my turn.

Earlier in the year, I had passed the written exam for my private pilot's license and began my formal flight instruction in the Piper PA-12. That was not to say I had never piloted this airplane. As I approached my teens, Dad often let me pilot the airplane once we were airborne. I could not see the instruments from the backseat, but I was familiar with the weight on the stick and the aircraft's response to the control input. Until I had turned 14, my legs had been too stubby to reach the rudder pedals or brakes, so I learned those later.

I was eager to fly on my own and when I was finally given the green flag to solo, I was more than ready to fulfill the formality. I remember the day well. After completing several circuits around the Soldotna airport, my instructor told me to taxi clear of the active runway. With the engine still idling, he opened the door and climbed out.

"You're ready. Take it around!" My instructor had said through the blast of propwash.

Then, with a laugh, he slammed the door, gave me a quick wave, and walked away.

I was ecstatic. For weeks, I had been chomping at the bit to be on my own and achieve what I had dreamed of ever since I was a child. The solo circuit around the airport was easy and I was quickly back in front of the airport office. My instructor officially entered this achievement into my flight logbook. Even with this documentation, I was still supposed to get approval from him to fly outside the local area; those parameters got stretched from time to time.

I blamed that on Dad. As far as he was concerned, I was now a pilot and when we went hunting, two planes were better than one; and because he had two planes, he let me fly one or the other—even when traveling 100 miles out of the local area into the mountain wilderness to the west. On those trips, my informal training continued. I flew in formation with Dad, watching him land and following him down like a fledgling imitating the adult; this was immensely valuable training. All the same, and as eager as I was to log hours, I left no trace of it in my logbooks.

Today, we would take one airplane, the PA-12, which was equipped with skis for winter operations. We were flying less than 30 minutes to the north and planned to be back by dark. The weather was agreeable for this time of year. The high, thin overcast to the south heralded the approach of another storm, but the clouds had kept the overnight temperatures from dropping to sub-zero. The air was still. It was a great day to hunt—and we were ready to go.

The pre-warmed engine whirled to life at the push of a button. After the engine had run for a minute or two, Dad advanced the throttle. We slipped and slid on the snow to the homestead strip and departed to the north.

There was no need to climb above 1,500 feet. We were not crossing open water, and with the lakes frozen, there were numerous places to land if an emergency occurred. After 15 minutes, we were beyond the only road that penetrated the north-central part of the Kenai Peninsula. Access to this area was by aircraft only.

We descended to 800 feet and began circling lakes that were large enough on which to land. With snow on the ground and no leaves on the foliage, it was easy to spot the dark form of a moose. Only cow moose, illegal to hunt, were in proximity to the first few lakes. Then we spotted antlers—a large bull, easily accessible, in the brush about two hundred yards off the northeast end of a lake. Another moose, apparently a cow, lay within a few yards of him.

Dad set up the approach from the south. Since there was no wind, he chose to stay as far away from the moose as possible. He did not want it to spook and run off. After touching down on the snow-covered lake, he switched off the engine, and we glided to a stop. The only sound was a slight squeaking of snow beneath the skis.

We did not say much. We had hunted together often and knew the drill. We exited the airplane as unobtrusively as possible, taking only the .300 H&H magnum with us. I had already loaded three rounds into the magazine and had a couple more in my pocket. Dad had the rest of the box of 20 shells in his jacket. The four to five inches of soft snow muted the shuffling of our feet. We worked our way silently beyond the end of the lake and into the thin, head-high brush. Farther in, there was heavier brush and some spruce trees; nevertheless, we had seen the moose in the more open area, on this side of the denser vegetation.

We paused to survey the scattered openings between the clumps of tall, spindly, gray stalks. From the air, it had looked a lot more open.

"I think we are close," whispered Dad over his shoulder.

"I agree," I said in a similar whisper.

I was packing the rifle, and he signaled for me to take the lead. I kept my eyes forward. We continued our advance. After another 100 feet, a slight movement caught my attention. I halted, then crouched. Dad followed my example. I pointed ahead. Dad nodded, understanding that I had seen something. Carefully, I chambered a round. We slowly rose and focused straight ahead. Once again, we pushed forward. In other situations, we would have kept as low a profile as possible, but in this case, we were in tall brush and needed as much height as we could to see. Being six-foot-five instead of my five-foot-six would have been beneficial.

Within a few more feet, I saw more motion. We were about 150 yards from a bull. It was not nearly as large as the one we had spotted from the air, but it had antlers, and that was all that mattered. We were here to fill the freezer, not hang something on the wall. I raised the rifle to my shoulder. I centered the crosshairs behind its front shoulder and squeezed the trigger. My ears rang from the shot and the moose dropped from view.

I did it. Simple. It was a satisfying feeling.

Without saying a word, Dad grinned.

The hunt was not yet finished, and we still needed to be silent because the big bull we had seen from the air remained in the area. We had a chance at getting the second animal, something that would top off the freezer and also provide meat to share with friends.

I replaced the spent cartridge with a fresh one and we carefully pushed through the brush toward the location of the fallen moose. Unexpectedly, a moose popped up about 75 yards out! A bull. I was baffled. How did the moose have the strength to flee when it heard us approach? I raised the rifle to my shoulder, quickly set up the shot, and fired. The animal dropped. I chambered another round just in case it sprang to life. Dad and I stared at each other wordlessly.

"I thought it was a good shot," I said, perplexed that the bull was still alive.

He shrugged his shoulders. Like me, he figured the two shots had scared the big bull off by now.

But then, the big bull stood up! I glanced at Dad and handed the rifle toward him. He motioned for me to keep it.

"Take the shot!" he whispered urgently.

Technically, he should have made the shot, but we had two moose tags and were legally covered in that regard.

Once again, I raised the rifle to my shoulder. This shot would not be simple or easy. The moose was walking away from us, and I did not have the angle I needed for a shot that wouldn't damage a hind quarter. At least it was a close shot—and the animal was not running. I fired. The animal did not drop immediately…why not? I had heard the slap of the shot striking the animal and knew I had hit it. Unbelievably, the big moose disappeared into the brush ahead of us.

"That was a solid shot. He will probably lie down and bleed out," said Dad.

"Yeah, I'd hate to see him run off, wounded like that," I replied.

Dealing with one issue at a time, we tread through the snow searching, for the first moose I had downed.

Sure enough, we found it a short distance away. Quite dead. When we reached the carcass, there was a complication. Within a few feet of that animal lay a second moose with identical racks. It was then we realized what had happened. There were three bulls in the brush, two similar in size, and the large bull we had identified from the air. What I had thought was the first moose experiencing the resurrection was actually its twin rising up. My emotions whiplashed from exuberance to dread. I was not worried about the two moose lying there; the third was the issue. The penalties for taking an extra moose in those days, while not nearly as draconian as they are now, could still be painful.

"What are we going to do?" I asked Dad.

"Let's check on that other bull," he suggested. "Maybe it wasn't hit too badly."

I was not as optimistic. "Yeah, maybe."

We quickly picked up a trail of blood, and within another 100 yards, we found the third bull, under a spruce tree, fatally wounded. We now knew what we had to deal with.

There were really only three options: report the extra moose, abandon it, or find a third person with a tag to claim it. I looked at Dad, the problem-solver.

"I pulled the trigger, so this is my fault," I stated.

"Leaving the third moose is not an option," said Dad.

I agreed with him on that point.

As I'd anticipated, a plan had already germinated in Dad's mind. "I'll tell you what. I'll stay here and dress out the moose. You fly home, find someone with a tag, and then fly him back out. What do you think?"

"Sure, I can do that," I replied confidently, regarding flying out and back in, but not necessarily in finding someone with a tag.

"Maybe Leonard Olson," Dad added.

I was relieved he'd thought of a tagger, which didn't really surprise me. Dad always had a plan.

"Leave me the rifle. I already have the knives with me," Dad instructed.

Back at the airplane, we pulled out a packboard, the lunch sack, and the emergency rations on board—not that there was much more than a Hershey's chocolate bar. Then we tugged the engine cover off the nose of the airplane, where we had hastily thrown it before we started stalking the moose. It was not a tent, but it would provide some shelter if worse came to worst. Dad also had matches to start a fire.

"Okay, you had best get going," he said, lifting the gear over his shoulder.

It was around noon, and at that time of year the sun appeared to grudgingly drag its feet as it climbed slowly above the horizon. Conversely, it seemed eager to retreat once it got there. The high, thickening clouds diminished the available light.

Dad disappeared back into the brush where a couple of tons of moose awaited him. I started the engine, applied power, and used the rudder pedals to bring the tail around. I pointed the plane back the way we had flown earlier, advanced the throttle to full power, and was soon airborne. After circling the lake once and seeing Dad industriously dressing out the first moose, I pointed the PA-12 homeward.

On the way back, I sure hoped Leonard would be available and could help with the moose situation. Otherwise, how was I going to set this up? I was raised to defer to adults and felt awkward in situations like this. I was a pilot and hunter, albeit younger, yet I was required to deal with adult pilots and hunters as peers.

I was still pondering this when I reached the homestead and landed. I taxied back to the hangar, shut down the engine, and ran to the house.

185

Mom had heard the airplane pull up to the hangar and was waiting at the top of the stairs when I burst through the front door.

"We have a problem!" I said, trying to catch my breath.

Alarm registered in her eyes.

"Where's Dad?" she blurted out instinctively.

"No, no! Dad's okay, but I shot a moose." I tried to rush the story and had trouble painting the correct picture.

Mom appeared confused. "You shot a moose."

"No, I mean, yes," I replied, still muddying the water with my urgency.

Mom twiddled her thumbs, something she did when anxious, and waited for me to gather my wits.

"I mean, we, uh, I shot three moose." My brain and mouth started to connect.

"They are all bulls," I continued. I didn't want Mom to think I had committed the unforgivable sin of shooting a cow moose.

"Dad stayed behind to dress out the moose and sent me back here to find someone to tag the third moose."

Mom thought briefly, then walked back to the kitchen and washed her hands before picking up the phone. I felt considerable relief that Mom would shoulder the responsibility for talking to adults. All the same, I fidgeted as she made phone calls. I was impatient and wanted to get back to help Dad. Finally, she hung up the phone.

"Leonard has a tag. He will grab a coat and head this way."

"Great!" I exclaimed. It was all going to work out.

"Tell me what happened," Mom said, motioning toward the kitchen table.

Mom made me a sandwich while I slumped wearily at the table. "Mom, it happened like this…."

About 30 minutes later, Leonard Olson pulled up in front of the house with his red three-quarter-ton Chevy pickup.

Mom and I greeted him at the door and nearly yanked him inside. The thickly built Swede wore a heavy coat and a trapper's hat. The hat was essential in keeping his mostly bald head warm. He was prepared. A pilot himself, he knew small airplanes had little heat and some were quite drafty. The waning daylight urged me to get back to Dad. We said goodbye to Mom, headed out the door, and walked toward the hangar.

"Where's Doc?" Leonard asked, casually looking around.

"He's with the moose, all of them," I replied.

Leonard did not precisely stop walking, but I saw him blink and process that information.

"So, who's flying?"

"I am," I said. "Unless you want to."

I threw out the last comment in deference. He was an adult, and I was a kid.

He thought about it momentarily; then, a thin smile spread across his face. "Oh, no. You go ahead."

With that agreement, we climbed aboard and settled into our seats. Before starting the engine, I looked back over my shoulder and asked, "You have your tag?"

"Right here," he responded, patting a coat pocket.

And with that, I started the engine, and we were soon headed north.

A slight breeze had risen, pushing fog and low clouds in from the northwest. We had expected to be home before the storm arrived, but I was now worried the deteriorating weather would prevent us from reaching Dad. By the time we were 10 miles from the lake, or so I estimated, I had to duck under the clouds. Even at this low altitude, and with no precipitation falling, visibility was still excellent. Flying was not difficult, yet I had to weave around hills of 600 to 700 feet scattered around the lakes.

After several minutes I failed to locate the lake where I had shot the moose, and I widened the search pattern. I knew I had to be close, but the appearance of the lakes, trees, and hills differed at this lower altitude, and the clouds prevented me from climbing higher to gain a better perspective. The flight of 30 minutes grew into 40. Then 50. I still could not find the lake. Leonard had not been to this spot and could not offer assistance except to look for the moose kills. The gas gauge hanging from the wing caught my attention. I was getting low on fuel. I swiveled my head toward Leonard and yelled above the engine noise.

"I need to get some gas."

He nodded in response, and I headed back south.

There was no fog back at the homestead and I swiftly landed and taxied to the hangar to add 10 gallons of gas. That would give me two hours of flight time. Daylight was fading and I would have to be back within two hours to beat the darkness anyway.

Mom showed up within minutes, her hastily thrown-on parka unzipped.

"I heard a plane land, but no one came to the house," she said with alarm.

"I can't find Dad," I told her, standing on a gear leg and balancing a can of gas on the wing.

"Dear Jesus," she prayed audibly. Her eyes filled with tears, and I knew she was thinking the worst.

"We'll find him, Ruby," Leonard told her as he reached to take the empty gas container and heft a full one up to me.

"Mom, I had to get some more gas. We're going back out. Right away. He has the rifle and some emergency gear, just in case...."

I emptied the second can and hopped down.

Leonard and I pushed the tail around, climbed in, and I waved at Mom, who waited for me to start the engine. I knew she would head back to the house and spend some time praying for us. I pressed the starter button yet again and we were on our way.

The conditions to the north had not changed, and I was back under the clouds again. All the lakes still looked the same. Though I knew each one was unique, there was enough similarity to confuse me. The map, though highly accurate, was of little use since the lakes shown were so small. Besides, I had no idea which lake on the map corresponded to the one Dad was on. I decided to head farther east and look at the lakes there. As I made a pass around one, I spotted something shadowy on the edge. I pulled the plane around to get a better look. There was Dad! With a sigh of relief, I circled back to make my landing.

After touching down, I taxied over to Dad, shut off the engine, and Leonard and I climbed out.

"Good to see you," said Dad. Looking directly at me, he continued, "A bit tricky, isn't it? The country all starts looking the same."

"It sure does," I agreed.

Leonard and Dad pulled off their gloves and shook hands. Dad led us to the edge of the lake.

"Here are the three moose. I have them quartered, stacked, and covered the best I can," Dad explained. He turned to Leonard. "Leonard, you have a tag?"

"Sure do, Doc." He pulled the tag from his coat pocket and handed it to Dad. Dad walked over to the stacks of moose meat and placed it beneath one of the upper pieces.

"Okay, let's go home," he said. "It's getting dark. We will fly the meat out later."

As we returned to the airplane, he told me what was going through his mind while I had been gone. "I heard you off to the west earlier and thought you might be having trouble with the fog that blew in. I was just getting ready to spend the night when you showed up."

Dad claimed the front seat while Leonard and I buckled in behind him. Before long, we were on approach to the homestead airstrip. We had barely beat the darkness but were back in plenty of time for supper.

We were fortunate I was able to rescue Dad. The weather closed in that night, and we were unable to retrieve the moose meat for three days. When we returned, wolves had scavenged some of the meat. It was just as well Dad had not been stuck there.

CHAPTER 12
STICKY SITUATIONS

EARLY IN SEPTEMBER, when the leaves had turned golden and the calm water of the lakes mirrored their beauty, Dad remarked to me, "Let's see if we can get some geese. I heard they were gathering on the flats by Chickaloon."

He had hunted ducks and geese by boat but never by flying and landing. And, the J-3 was still on floats, ready to go.

"Sure. I'll tag along," I replied. "What do the tides look like?"

Dad had not asked if I wanted to go along. It was understood that I would. I loved flying. The sensation of large tundra tires rolling on sandy beaches bouncing over rocky gravel bars or watching snow blossom behind skis on a frozen lake, or splashing down on floats continued to give me pleasure.

"Looks like a minus tide around 2 p.m. So, we will want to land by 10 to catch the tide when it's up a ways."

The quick 30-mile trip to the flats, at the north end of the Kenai Peninsula, across from Anchorage, would not require extra fuel or overnight gear. Waterfowl pause in this area, along the south edge of the Turnagain Arm, on their migration to warmer climates. It was only a 30-minute jaunt and since we were leaving before noon, we figured we could hunt for a couple hours and be back home by suppertime.

We hopped into the car and drove out to the J-3 on Sports Lake. At age 16, I had grown into a full participant in flying and worked alongside Dad; in this case, I pumped out residual water from the floats. After completing this and other tasks, I stood in the swampy shallows of the lake in my hip boots and held onto the airplane's tail while Dad grabbed the prop and pulled it through. The engine fired immediately and settled into a smooth idle. Dad folded himself into the front seat. With a gentle push, I stepped onto a float and the plane pulled away from the shore. We fastened our seatbelts, and Dad completed the pre-takeoff checklist.

He slipped the throttle, and we skimmed along the lake's even surface. The lightly loaded J-3 jumped into the air, and we headed north. Dad chose to fly under 1,000 feet, not because the weather demanded it, but because we both instinctively scouted for moose. If either of us spotted something of interest, we would draw attention to it.

Before long, we saw the end of the Peninsula. Dad avoided flying directly over the area we intended to hunt yet getting just close enough to confirm that plenty of ducks and geese were clustered in the shallow ponds that dotted the marsh. He then looked for a place to land.

Our previous float flying had been on freshwater. That meant our concerns had been the length of the lake, obstacles to clear, wave height, debris in the water, river width and current, and finding a rock-free place to beach the aircraft. Here, there were threats of corrosive salt water and moving tides. And mud. The mud along Turnagain Arm and parts of Cook Inlet is composed of extremely fine silt particles. It is notoriously sticky—and fickle. A myriad of salty streams that cut into the muddy banks carry the cold, briny water back and forth with the tides, tides that can vary 30 feet between high and low. It was in this watery environment that Dad set down the J-3.

With only the usual caution, Dad taxied up one of the broader turbid tidal streams that ended in a shallow muddy bank about a mile from the marshes we wanted to hunt. Switching the engine off, he let the airplane coast slowly up to the bank.

He climbed out and leaped nimbly off the float, then held onto the prop to steady the plane while I exited. Wordless and intent, he examined the muddy beach. This was not at all like the sandy or grassy beaches to which we were accustomed.

"I don't think we can get it turned around to tie it off," he said.

"Sure doesn't look that way, does it," I replied.

"Well, grab that stake out of the back, and we can tie the nose of a float to that," he said. "We won't be gone very long anyway."

He pounded the stake into the drier mud above the current waterline and roped the airplane to it. I pulled the lightweight aluminum, bare-frame packboards from the baggage compartment. With packs on our backs, Dad shouldered his 16-gauge pump shotgun, and we were off.

There were no trails to follow. For the first few hundred yards, we walked on firm ground where scattered tufts of knee-high grass poked up here and there. This was doable. As we worked our way toward the ponds, where we had seen the geese, taller grass snatched at our hip boots, and our boots frequently sank into soft, wet spots. Occasionally, pools of water too deep to cross blocked our progress. We searched for different routes through what was becoming a maze. I felt uneasy. The marsh grasses were now over waist-high, with more water than dry ground.

What do you think? We about halfway there?" Dad asked.

"Could be," I responded. "Too hard to tell in all this tall grass."

We continued for a few more minutes, and after yet another dead end, he admitted defeat. "This isn't going to work. Let's go back."

"That's fine with me," I said. I had been ready to turn back a half-hour earlier.

Going back was easier since we could avoid the dead ends. After a half-hour, we spied the J-3 and adjusted our course to intercept it. As we got closer, something looked off. The plane sat at a peculiar angle. I did not recall the nose pointing that high when we had left.

"The plane sure is sitting funny," I remarked without breaking stride. "I hope something didn't hole a float or something." I didn't want to lose our ride out of here.

"Huh," was all Dad said and picked up the pace. He had seen this, too.

When we arrived at the aircraft, the reason was startlingly apparent. The tide had gone out, and the J-3 now rested on the slanted muddy bank. The wide, murky channel we had taxied up was a mere trickle.

Dad cleared his throat. "Looks like we are going to be here a while."

He did not seem dejected. It was just an observation. It would take much more to cause Dad to despair.

The waterline was hundreds of yards away with glistening mud for miles in either direction. There was nothing we could do except wait for the tide to return. With a couple of hours to kill, we sat on the floats and talked about homestead things, nothing of much consequence, just something to hold apprehension at bay.

"I think we need to get in a bit more firewood before winter," Dad said.

I drew circles in the damp mud with a small stick. "It's getting hard to find dead trees that aren't already down."

"We may have to go back into the woods, farther west along the runway."

"Yeah, but that's a lot of work." We had done that before.

After three long hours, the tide finally turned, and its leading-edge advanced rapidly. We watched the grimy water approach the mucky banks.

When it reached the back of the floats, we untied the plane and loaded our gear. We expected to see the J-3 rise from the mud, buoyed by the water. Instead, it remained motionless, with the water slowly creeping up the floats' sides. The sludge had the airplane in its grip.

"We need to rock it free," Dad shouted urgently. "Grab a wing!"

We each got under a wing as best we could and tried to wrestle the floats free. No success. Pushing on the wings only drove our boots farther into the entrapping mire.

"Can we dig the mud out?" I yelled. Neither of us had ever experienced anything like this and we were grasping at straws.

For several minutes, we tried this tactic; however, with only our small aluminum paddle, we made slight headway. The water inched over the back of the floats. The hatch covers on top of the float compartments were not watertight, and if submerged, the compartments would slowly flood. We faced the very chilling possibility we might not get the airplane free, and if so, it would be sunk by the incoming tide and then torn apart by the outgoing tide.

I had been positioned alongside one of the floats and in our attempt to lift the airplane, I had not noticed my hip boots working their way farther and farther into the mud. I tried to step toward the front of the floats to escape the rising water. I couldn't. Water splashed over the tops with my boots lodged firmly below the surface.

"I'm stuck!" I cried out.

Dad was dealing with similar issues on his side and did not respond. My mind leaped to stories I had heard of people trapped in the same quicksand along Cook Inlet. People had been swallowed by the water and mud and drowned by the rising tide. I did not want to die like that.

I unsnapped my bootstraps, pulled out my feet, and scrambled onto the floats. From there, I could lean over, wrestle my boots loose, and slip them back on. While I had been struggling, Dad had managed to get unstuck while keeping his boots on.

The water had now risen over the back three feet of the floats' length and was too deep for us to stand alongside the floats, so we moved up the bank by the plane's nose. The incoming water did not stop.

The entire flats we had hiked were rapidly disappearing under the incoming tide. At this point, we could not save the J-3, and it could not save us, or could it? When it comes to a search and rescue operation, pilots are told to stay with their downed plane since it is easier to spot than a person. Maybe we could crawl up on the wings and hope the tide did not rip the plane apart and drag us down with it. Probably not a good bet. But if we abandoned the J-3, where could we go? We were more than a mile out in a vast tidal flat, a tidal flat that would soon be under water. Not just a few inches, either.

Before we left the house, Dad had said it was a minus tide, meaning the low tide would be lower than normal. It also meant the incoming high tide would be higher than normal. Where we stood watching the tide rush in, we could end up under four feet of icy water. Even if the current did not sweep us away, it was doubtful we could survive in the frigid water for four hours or more, waiting for the tide to switch and recede.

There were no good solutions. All we could do now was stand on the shrinking island of grass by the nose of the airplane and wait for the inevitable.

Then the floats did what we couldn't. Their buoyancy finally overcame the suction of the mud, and not unlike a breaching whale, popped to the surface with a rush of water. I heard the words, "Thank you, Lord," repeatedly. It may have been Dad or may have been me. Probably both.

As wet and muddy as we had become in our efforts to save the plane, we clambered onto the floats and aboard the orange aircraft. Dad propped the engine to life and immediately pointed the J-3 toward deeper water. Then he pushed the throttle forward, and we winged our way back home.

Back at Sports Lake, we splashed water on the floats to clean off the muddy, salty reminder of our sticky situation. How fortunate we had been. While we did not bag any geese, getting home in one piece was a remarkable success in itself.

So ended our one and only airborne goose hunt.

That was not the only time we tangled with Cook Inlet silt. When I was 17, Dad decided to inspect the property he had purchased along the northwest coast of the Kenai Peninsula. The Kenai Peninsula Borough had auctioned off parcels ranging from two to seven acres in an area designated as Grey Cliffs Subdivision with the idea of putting more land into private hands.

At the time, there was no road to these parcels, and access during the summer was primarily by ATV slopping down a muddy trail. As is the case in any area, lots with a view are the most desirable, and Dad had bid on some lots that provided unobstructed views of the Aleutian Range to the west. It also meant this was beachfront property. Pilots like beaches. Especially sandy beaches. They provide a place to operate airplanes. Unfortunately, Dad was outbid on the lot he had his eye on and ended up with a plot with a view—and a rocky beach. Not only that, but the beach was also below a 30-foot ocean-eroded bluff.

"This is not all that bad," Dad told me. "The beach farther out is rock-free."

"That means we can only land at low tide." I countered my always-confident father.

Dad had worked the angles and ignored the implications of my comment. "We could land out there and taxi up the beach and wind our way among the bigger rocks until we are close to the bottom of the bluff of our property."

One Saturday in December, with clear weather and a daylight window of five hours, he decided to test this theory. The temperature had peaked in the mid-teens and hesitated there in anticipation of following the sun downward. Local lakes were locked in five to six inches of ice and topped with a layer of thin, crunchy snow. Since the snow cover in general was still sparse, Dad had not changed the J-3 over to skis and it still sat on large tires.

These were not as big as the tall, fat "tundra" tires often associated with Alaska bush airplanes. However, on the lightweight Piper, they provided sufficient flotation on any soft beach sand we might customarily encounter.

We launched from the homestead airstrip as we had done hundreds of times before. Twenty-five minutes later, Dad circled the property at 1,000 feet. I could make out the wiggly white line, which marked the summer trail that would soon provide access by snow machine. The bluff property supported stands of birch and isolated spruce trees. The underbrush, now bare of leaves like the trees, consisted primarily of thin patches of willow, highbush cranberries, alders, and an occasional clump of thorny Devil's club, the latter of which could make life miserable for the unwary. Several small, frozen lakes gathered approximately a mile inland from the bluff. Dad aimed the airplane back over the beach to scrutinize the chosen landing site. The tide had retreated well enough away from this patch of sand, and a low flyby revealed no rocks of any size. I noticed that some of the sand appeared to glisten, while in other places, it was dull. Any implications of this did not cross my mind. With his assessment completed, Dad swung the plane around, pulled the throttle back, and set up the approach to land. There was little wind, and the J-3 settled gently onto the sand. It was just another ordinary landing…until…the wheels sank into…what was this? Mud! This was completely unanticipated and brought the airplane to a sudden stop. Fortunately, it did not flip onto its nose, something that can happen when the front wheels dig in.

Dad switched off the engine.

"Where did *that* come from?" I exclaimed.

"It sure didn't look like this from the air," Dad said. "Let's get out and take a look."

Misadventures seemed to lurk like stowaways in the baggage compartment of Dad's airplanes, but at least this time we were not in a life-threatening situation. The worst that could happen was the tide would submerge the silt-stuck airplane while we watched helplessly from the safety of higher ground, which was accessible.

We climbed out of the airplane and stepped into the mud with our snow boots, not rubber boots, designed for mud and water. Nevertheless, the snow boots provided a broader footprint, and we pressed onto the soft ground rather than sinking in deeply. We walked back along the tire tracks to where we had touched down. How had we been fooled? Then we solved the mystery: some areas of mud were frozen, and others were not. What I had observed from the air had provided the clue. The dull sections were frozen, and the shiny ones were not. We had rolled into one of the unfrozen patches and sunk.

"Well, okay. Where is the closest frozen piece of beach?" I asked.

It proved to be 75 feet in front of us. Out in that area, we paced off the distance needed to takeoff, 150 feet. What we had was under 100.

"We are going to have to lighten the plane," Dad stated. "One of us has to stay behind, rock the plane free, and help push it to the frozen mud for takeoff."

Even though I had enough experience to fly the J-3, I was unwilling to accept the responsibility. Besides, Dad had a lot more experience extracting himself from self-inflicted predicaments.

"It's your plane. I'll stay behind. Where will you pick me up?"

"You saw the lake straight east of here?"

I nodded.

"Head straight for that and I'll wait for you there."

He climbed into the J-3, and I walked to the front of the plane.

I grabbed the tip of the prop with both hands and pulled it down briskly. The engine fired and caught. Walking back to the wing tip, I got under the strut and waited for Dad to add power. With me no longer in the back seat, the airplane only weighed around 1,000 pounds. When I heard the engine speed increase, I rocked the wing. Dad pushed the control stick forward and the tail raised enough to clear the mud. Slowly, the airplane wallowed forward. I kept pace, moving the wing up and down. When we reached the frozen patch, the wheels rode up onto the harder surface. I let go of the wing. The airplane accelerated rapidly. It was airborne before reaching the end of the solid mud.

"Well, that wasn't too hard," I said to myself.

I watched the J-3 disappear over the trees and travel eastward. I understood that Dad was giving me the bearing to the lake, and I started out to meet him. It was about 150 yards to the base of the 30-foot bluff. Thirty feet may not be that high, but it was quite steep, and the last four feet were vertical. I could not scale those four feet, so I walked along the base for another 100 yards, until I found a notch cut into the bank by a now-frozen stream. Here, I managed to crawl to the top. If Dad was going to use this way up in the future, I would recommend a stout rope.

Once on top, I picked a landmark as a reference and set out across the scant snow. Trees hid the sun, which at that time of the year sat low on the horizon. Still, I could discern a southerly direction. From what I remembered of our flyover of the property before landing, I figured the rendezvous point was only a mile away, although a mile in unfamiliar territory can seem like a very long way. With a mental picture in my mind, I headed toward the lake. The terrain did not impede my progress. Snow had knocked down the deep grass, and there was little underbrush.

Even though I could keep a heading in the woods, staying on course took effort. After 15 to 20 minutes of hiking, I started to second-guess myself. Had I missed the lake? Would Dad take off and come looking for me? Why was the compass in the emergency gear on the plane, instead of in my pocket? Was that an airplane I heard? Yes. Very high up. Not the J-3.

After a while, the brush gave way to a wall of evergreens. I had noted when we flew over, that trees grew more densely around this lake's shoreline, so I must be close. Having faith without sight and energized by the hope that the lake would soon appear, I pushed the boughs aside and wormed my way forward. Sure enough, I broke out of the forest and onto the frozen swamp bordering the lake.

Like a beacon, the orange J-3, a hundred yards away, rewarded me for my determination and efforts. Dad stood beside the plane, facing my direction. He must have heard the racket I made working through the dense trees and guessed it was me—or a bull moose. He waved. I waved back and walked faster.

When I approached him, Dad remarked, "Well, that wasn't too bad, was it?"

"You mean getting the plane out or me finding this lake?"

Dad grinned. "I didn't have any trouble. Did you?"

"Not really," I grinned, too.

"I didn't think you would. Hop in, and let's go home."

Twenty minutes later, we taxied to the hangar, and Dad shut down the engine. We climbed out, secured the airplane, and walked to the house.

"Nice day to be out, wasn't it," Dad commented.

The way he said it made me feel like a peer rather than just a kid.

"Yeah, pretty nice," I agreed, with a grin on my face.

The J-3 was home safely, but the mud splattered on the bottom of the wings, where the tires had thrown the muck, was a reminder of the treachery that awaited the unwary.

CHAPTER 13
CAMP INOWAK

I CHECKED THE OIL of the PA-12 and wiped the residue off the dipstick.

An 11-year-old girl with long, dark brown hair pulled neatly into a ponytail walked up with a sleeping bag in her arms.

I smiled and said, "Hi Jan, you ready to go?"

"I think so."

"You don't sound very sure," I teased.

That brought a shy grin.

Her dad, Tommy Dwinnell, who was also a pilot, watched me go through my preflight routine. The burly, barrel-chested man had been a hockey player. Not only that, he was a hunter and could pack out a quarter of moose without much effort, something Dad and I appreciated when we went out with him.

"Hi, Mark. Looks like good weather for the trip, eh?" He was Canadian.

"Yep, pretty good."

The fact that I was only 18 years old and was flying his daughter cross-country didn't seem to bother him at all. He knew Dad and had watched me grow up as a homestead kid and the son of a respected bush pilot.

"Here are the rest of Jan's things," he said, with a duffle bag in one hand.

"Just set them over there." I motioned to a spot nearby and completed my inspection of the aircraft. Dad showed up with a brown paper grocery bag, handed it to me, and started chatting with Tommy. I peered inside and saw a cabbage, apples, and a bunch of carrots. Mom must have sent him a shopping list.

I had already loaded my gear: a sleeping bag, extra clothes, a fishing rod, emergency gear, which included a .357 revolver, and a guitar. Jan's duffle fit next to my belongings in the baggage compartment. The grocery bag filled another spot. The plane filled up quickly.

"I'll put your sleeping bag on the seat next to you," I told Jan.

She nodded. Since the PA-12 seated two people on the rear bench seat, there was plenty of room for her, plus the sleeping bag.

The last items to load were two cans of aviation gas and a large funnel with a chamois filter.

All this preparation was for a trip to Camp Inowak (Een-a-WOK), a summer camp for Native kids. The Penz family, who had started the camp, had once worked for MARC and had lived in our cabin. A number of people from our church were acquainted with them and subsequently volunteered to help with the camp, including my mom, who was quite capable of cooking for large groups. And her recipes were carefully chosen to bring smiles to the staff and children.

The camp was located on an oxbow lake, formed when a bend in the Kuskokwim had been cut off from the main channel by a natural change in the waterway. This lake lay between the villages of Stony River and Sleetmute.

Every June, dozens of kids attended the camp. Most were flown in from the villages, although a few arrived in their small boats. My job was to lead music with my guitar and help with miscellaneous camp chores. Jan planned to assist Mom, who had flown over a few days earlier to help set up the camp.

At over 300 miles to the west of our homestead, it was a long trip in the PA-12; long enough to require additional fuel for the return flight. There were no airports along the route to refuel. The two five-gallon cans of the gas I'd wrestled directly behind the rear seat were my ticket home.

"I'm ready. Let's go," I announced.

Tommy helped Jan into the rear seat. I made sure her seatbelt was fastened before I climbed up to the single seat in the front. The men stood clear of the airplane, and I pulled the door shut. Before I proceeded further, I did what Dad always did before he departed on a long flight. I turned to my passenger and said, "Let's pray." Jan nodded. I removed my hat and bowed my head.

"Lord, please give us good weather and a safe journey today. In Jesus' name, Amen."

Then I donned my hat, primed the engine, switched on the magnetos, checked again to make sure no one was in front of the prop, yelled "Clear," and pushed the starter button. The prop spun through a rotation and the engine coughed to life. The oil pressure indicator settled into the green and I waited for the engine to warm up. Under the watchful eyes of the dads, I taxied down our grassy runway and departed to the north.

I had finally gained my pilot's license just a couple of months prior to this flight but had already accumulated a significant number of hours as pilot-in-command, not to mention hundreds of hours in the back seat with Dad at the controls. The previous summer, I had made this same trip with him, so I had a good idea of how the flight should go. I had offered to take Jan on this flight and the two dads had agreed. Even though their endorsement had reinforced my confidence, I felt the added responsibility of a passenger.

Forty-five minutes into the flight, we reached the entrance to Merrill Pass, which cut through the southern end of the Alaska Range and was more in line with our destination than Lake Clark Pass farther south. Unlike the broad, low pass of Lake Clark, Merrill rises from a few hundred feet above sea level to a high point of about 3,200 feet. At the summit, it narrows, and the rock wall on the south side thrusts into the canyon. Here it is too narrow for an airplane to abort and turn around. I climbed to 4,500 feet, still below the peaks, but high enough to clear the summit and avoid the mountainside that jutted into the pass. As we approached the highpoint, grim reminders of airplanes that had not made it through lay scattered on the tundra-covered valley floor, and even on the sides: twisted airframes and lines of metal debris. I glanced behind me. Jan was peering at this graveyard, too.

After another 20 minutes, the ground slowly fell away, leaving the mountains behind us. All the same, I held my altitude constant. Before us stretched the Kuskokwim River basin, and beyond that, the Yukon River. I tracked my progress with an FAA-approved sectional map. I had a radio, but it had no navigational aids. The weather on the west side of the Alaska Range is different from that on the east. The coolness of Cook Inlet on the east side reduces thermal heating and stifles the buildup of cumulus clouds. There is no such moderating influence on the west side, and the heat of the day causes puffy clouds to form and grow. If the airmass is unstable, thundershowers are common, and while thunderstorms were not in the forecast, I wanted to be at our destination before afternoon rain showers interfered with visibility.

Out on the flats, small lakes lay sprinkled across large stretches of swamp, in a pattern that ran to the horizon. It was easy for a pilot to become confused. As accurate as the map was, it did not show every water feature. The trick was to find larger lakes, perhaps a half mile across, and match their shape with a similar shape on the map. I used these to confirm checkpoints along my route. The compass only helped in a general sense. With 23 degrees of magnetic deviation, north on the map and north on the compass were in different directions.

In this area, there were no places to make an emergency landing, no sandy ocean beaches, or significant river bars. I checked the instruments often and listened to the loud drone of the motor, alert for any hint of trouble. I was pretty sure we could survive an emergency landing, but in this hostile country, surviving the mosquitoes would be another issue. People complained about them back home on the Kenai Peninsula, but those mosquitoes were wimpy compared to the clouds of blood-sucking pests that swarmed the Interior during June. And this was June.

It was 100 miles from where I had left the mountains to where I intended to intersect the Kuskokwim River. The scattered clouds began to develop dark bottoms as they gathered moisture and became heavy. Here and there thin veils of rain hung down. I dodged around them while maintaining my general heading.

The Kuskokwim had to be ahead…somewhere…. Several minutes passed. I checked my watch. According to the elapsed time from my last checkpoint, it should be in view. Then I saw it. Lofty spruce and birch trees along its banks had hidden it.

The river was about 10 miles away and I started a gradual descent. I looked back at my passenger. Given the din of the motor, there had been no conversation for over two and a half hours. Dad and I managed to communicate when hunting, but I doubted Jan's vocal cords were up to that kind of abuse. Instead, I pointed forward and nodded my head. She nodded hers in response. Now I had to find the mile-and-a-half-long oxbow lake and the gravel bar used as an airstrip.

My navigation had been quite accurate, and I crossed the 200-foot-wide river less than a mile from the lake. I corrected course slightly and continued to descend. Now that I had the crescent-shaped lake in sight, I knew the location of the camp. Before landing, I would circle the camp and let the staff know I had arrived. They knew I was coming since Dad's telephone call had been relayed to them via ham radio.

Five hundred feet below, I saw the camp in the trees. Green canvas tents were pitched along the perimeter of a cleared area that served as a sports field. Between them and the lake was the main meeting area and kitchen, both covered in clear plastic. A short distance away was a small log cabin. Even on my first pass, people came out in the open and waved. Like many other places in Alaska, people were keenly attuned to the sound of an airplane since that was the primary means of transportation in and out of the area. I completed a second pass, then pointed the airplane toward the river and the improvised runway.

I noticed the gravel bar landing strip was in the same spot as the previous year. That was not always the case. The river channel constantly shifted, and gravel bars appeared and disappeared. Village residents knew how to read the river and adjusted. To the uninitiated, it was frustrating or outright hazardous.

No other airplanes were on the gravel bar, and I circled to land. The usable section of the strip was maybe 1,500 feet long, plenty of distance for the PA-12. With the landing checklist completed, I reduced power and let the airspeed bleed off. It always felt unnerving to fly low over the water on an approach for a gravel bar landing. As the airplane crossed the riverbank, I pulled the throttle back to idle and let the airplane settle. The fat tundra tires kissed the gravel, and I braked to a stop.

I taxied to where the gravel bar was nearest the river and pulled into a line of willows along the edge. These would be my tie-downs. I killed the engine and sat in silence for a moment. It had been three hours and 15 minutes since we had left the homestead. It had not been a difficult flight, still, I felt the tension of piloting melt away.

Jan was eager to disembark, and I did not blame her. I helped her out and we stretched our cramped limbs. I pulled out a can of bug repellent and handed it to her.

"Here. You'll need this."

"Okay," she replied hesitantly. I read the skepticism on her face.

She sprayed her open palm and dabbed her face and neck before handing it back. I held the button down and gave my neck, face, shirt, pants, and hat a liberal blast. She stared at me aghast. The mosquitoes were not bad on this exposed gravel bar, where only a few dozen circled us, but hordes lurked expectantly in the brush, only a dozen yards away. I didn't say a word. This was her first trip into the Alaskan Interior, and she had not truly experienced mosquitoes. In a couple of hours, if not before, she would have a new understanding of the little vampires.

While we waited for someone to transport us to camp, I refueled the airplane; this required using a funnel and chamois. Few aromas make passengers queasier than fumes from a gas-soaked chamois. By tending this now, the chamois and funnel would have plenty of time to dry before the next flight.

Whoever was headed our way had to motor a mile down the lake, then navigate a small stream that drained the lake into the Kuskokwim. Underbrush hid the lake's exit, and our ride seemed to materialize out of thin air. The boatman sat in the back, hand on the tiller, and skillfully negotiated the swift current. He followed the wandering channel and avoided the shallows where the rocky bottom could instantly destroy the motor's propeller and leave him to drift helplessly downstream.

As he drew nearer, I recognized the boatman as Dave Penz, the camp founder and director. Dave was a bit more than six feet tall and broad-shouldered. He wore brown knee-high rubber boots common among people who lived along the river, and his forest-green duck-fabric jeans were paired with a brown plaid work shirt. A dark blue baseball hat topped his sandy-colored hair. He ran the bow onto the sandy edge of the gravel bar, and I steadied it as he jumped out. The boats used on the river were generally stable, flat-bottomed, shallow-draft watercraft, 16 to 20 feet long, powered by 25 to 40 hp outboard motors, referred to as "kickers." His was one such craft.

"Hi, Mark. Hello, Jan. Did you have a good trip?"

"Yep, we had great weather. No problems at all," I replied.

Without delay, we loaded our gear into the boat. On his signal, I pushed the boat back into the river and sprang aboard.

Until he eased into the calmer waters of the creek, Dave's attention remained focused on the roiling river water. As we slid past the tall grass along the banks, he gave us a run-down of the camp.

"The lake is higher this year, so we don't have to pull the boats up the creek."

I had participated in that effort the prior year and it was hard work. The mosquitoes did not help us either.

He continued, "Camp is set up. The kids will arrive tomorrow. I will be flying them in from Stony and Sleetmute. Two or three are coming from Red Devil, too."

Red Devil was a mining village downriver from Sleetmute.

"Mark, your mom was glad to see you buzz the camp. She has been praying for your flight over."

I smiled at that. Mom always prayed when Dad and I were in the air.

When we reached the lake, a few minutes later, Dave twisted the throttle and we surged across the water. As we approached the small dock, I saw

Mom standing at the top of the 20-foot-high bank, with her red-and-white woven wide-rimmed summer hat. I would have recognized her anywhere.

I offered my hand to Jan, and she disembarked from the slightly rocking boat.

"Just a second and I'll pass you your things," I said. "Then you can go ahead while I unload my gear."

With my sleeping bag in one hand, and guitar and bag of clothes in the other, I climbed the dirt trail up the bank. At the top, I set down my load and Mom hugged me. I had finally grown and passed Mom's five-foot, two-inches.

"It's so good to see you!" she said, beaming.

"It's good to see you, too, Mom," I said, and grinned.

"Come see my kitchen," she continued, her hand comfortably on my arm. "By the way, you will be with the 10-year-olds. I hope Charlie will be back this year. He followed you around like a puppy last year."

That was true. At camp, kids were surrounded by people who cared about them, and sometimes a little love resulted in instant bonding. This can be true of children anywhere; however, the villages were plagued with alcohol abuse, and as a result, many of the children suffered from a lack of kindness and attention. Here they felt safe.

Jan trailed after one of the older girls and I followed Mom toward the plastic-covered framework that served as a kitchen.

"Anyone new coming to help this year?" I asked.

"Well, a new couple is coming from McGrath."

McGrath lies along the Kuskokwim River, 100 miles to the northeast. With a population of around 400, it was one of the larger communities.

On our way to the camp, we were overtaken by Roger, a young man from our church. He and his wife Barb had been here last year, too.

"Hi Mark, I'll drop these groceries off for your mom, then I'll take you to your tent."

When we reached the makeshift kitchen, Mom pulled a plastic flap aside to let Roger enter. He set the bag on a wooden counter, and she thanked him.

Roger stepped back outside, and I turned to follow him.

"I'll be in the kitchen," Mom said, patting me on the shoulder. "Come tell me about your trip when you're settled in."

"Okay, I'll be back in a minute."

I followed Roger to the row of green tents in the boys' section.

"You'll be in this one. John will be in the next one. Glad you could help again this year. I see you brought a guitar."

"Well, Mom heard the camp needed someone to help with music, and she sort of volunteered me."

We both chuckled and he went on his way.

Through the flipped-up tent flaps, I could see the dirt floor. Inside, two rows of four canvas cots rested against the tent walls. I chose a cot nearest the door, unrolled my sleeping bag, and placed my bag on top. This was as clean as my clothes would be for the next two weeks.

Then, back to the kitchen, I went.

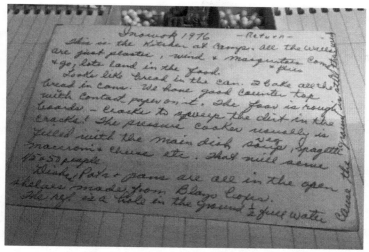

Ruby Gaede's Description of Her Camp Kitchen

A Volunteer, Ruby Gaede, and Jan Dwinnell in the Camp Kitchen

Lunch was over and supper was a few hours away, yet this did not mean Mom was sitting and sipping tea. For the camp cook, when one meal ended, another one began. Later, while kitchen volunteers dried the supper dishes, Mom would be planning the next day's breakfast.

Camp Inowak Recipe for Potato Omelet for 50 Campers

I pulled the plastic door aside, stepped in, and tightly closed the flap to keep the bugs out. Her back to me, Mom stood at the wooden counter and chopped celery, which she methodically plunked into a large metal pot on the propane stove.

She turned around and exclaimed, "Mark! Did you notice my new wood floor? So much nicer than standing on dirt like I did last year."

My mother was not one to complain. She saw the bright side of a situation, and in this case, she was grateful for the upgrade.

I acknowledged her improved working conditions, then asked, "What are you cooking?"

"Hamburger soup," she replied. She stirred the mixture, lifted the spoon clear of the pot, sampled the liquid dripping from the end, and made satisfied sounds.

"So. How was your trip?"

This question was so like Mom. She asked Dad the same thing when he returned from a flight or a hunt. Even as a kid, she would ask me about my expedition at the creek, fishing, or at a friend's house. As I grew older, her interest remained the same. On a trip like this, my adventures began to sound more and more like Dad's.

Leaning against the wood counter covered with contact paper, I launched into my flight debriefing.

"Oh, it was pretty nice. No clouds on the east side. Visibility was really good. Oh, we could see McKinley as soon as we started the climb out from the homestead. Not too many bumps except for some chop between Lime Village and here. Fortunately, not enough to make Jan sick."

I paused to watch her re-stir the pot, then I resumed.

"I had forgotten how wild that country is through the mountains and on this side, but the plane purred right along. We had a tailwind, so made really good time."

"I'm glad you had a good flight," she said. "That was an answer to my prayers. My flight last week with the MARC pilot was scary through Rainy Pass. Lots of rain and very bumpy.

I responded. "Yes, that pass can get weather, but it's not as rugged as Merrill."

Mom added more ingredients.

"Are you hungry? There's some coffee cake left from breakfast if you'd like some."

My eyes lit up. Even here in the wilderness, Mom could make delicious cinnamon-and-sugar-topped coffeecake.

"That sounds terrific! Thanks!"

She cut an ample square. "Would you like a glass of Tang, too?"

"That would be great."

Our conversation continued, and after a while, I asked how her first week at camp had gone.

"It rained every day," she said with a sigh. "You know Lucy, the young Native girl who is my assistant cook. Well, we sleep in a two-man tent, and the first night our sleeping bags were damp and so cold. But the second night, Dave gave us a little gas heater. That was such a blessing!"

I knew about cold, damp sleeping bags. At times, Dad decided a tent was too much weight in the plane, and when we hunted, we slept on the bare ground with leaky Visqueen plastic pulled over us.

My mom was no sissy. She had a passion for serving the Native people and would put up with all kinds of discomfort and inconveniences to do so, and in this case, it was for the Native children.

With my stomach's rumblings temporarily silenced, I left Mom and toured the camp. The camp sat on a low ridge, which was part of the original bank of the Kuskokwim. The river had wandered off and left this bend of the river isolated. One side of the ridge faced the lake. The other side fell into a draw with a narrow creek, which eventually dumped into the lake. This creek provided fresh water for the camp. There was a gasoline-powered water pump at the creek. When needed, it was fired up to fill a pair of 55-gallon drums sitting on stands outside the kitchen. Gravity then provided the kitchen with running water.

Like the kitchen, the meeting hall was constructed of a wood frame covered with plastic, although it had a dirt floor. Two long tables accommodated meals and crafts, and the campers and staff sat on rough-cut lumber benches. Singing and story time took place here, too.

To keep mosquitoes at bay, several smudge pots were posted on either side of the hall entrance and also outside the kitchen. The metal buckets containing smoldering wood embers were topped with green grass that produced a smokey curtain that pests were reluctant to pass.

By evening, around 20 staff volunteers from churches in Alaska, as well as Outside, had arrived, nearly equal to the campers they expected. The place buzzed with anticipation and excitement. Staff who had returned from the previous year caught up with one another, and first-timers were readily assimilated. Kitchen volunteers scurried to set tables, and a common phrase emerged: "Ruby Gaede makes the most delicious meals." In anticipation, people eagerly found seats. Before the volunteers served the meal, the camp director stood and asked us to bow our heads.

"Father, thank you for bringing this group of people together," he prayed. "Thank you for watching over them. We pray also for safety as we fly the kids in from the villages tomorrow. May this next week be special as we show them that we love them, and more importantly, that You love them. Bless this food and the hands that have prepared it. In Jesus' name, Amen."

After a murmur of "amens," the friendly conversation resumed.

I heard Mom's cheerful voice as she chatted with the servers carrying out bowls of hot soup. Jan was among them.

After supper, women cleared, washed, and dried dishes. I walked to the edge of the bluff above the dock. Two men, both wearing mosquito nets, were in the back of a boat tied to the dock. The kicker was tilted out to the water and one of the men pointed to the prop. I shuffle-slid down the bank to see what they were doing. I could hear their discussion.

"Looks like most of that third blade is gone," said one.

"That would explain the vibration and lack of oomph," said the other.

"I'm surprised it didn't take the shear pin."

One of them chuckled.

"What's going on?" I asked as I walked down the dock.

They looked up.

"Hi, Mark." one responded. Then they turned back to their work.

Here at the water, the mosquitoes droned in a frenzy. When I had descended the bank, I had attracted a personal entourage. Even though I'd saturated myself with bug dope, they persistently crawled into my ears and fluttered behind my glasses. I swatted constantly! This was no place to linger.

I watched the men work to remove the damaged propeller. The man closest to me had on a flannel shirt. It looked brownish-maroon, a rather odd color. Then he moved to reach a tool, and the shirt turned to a classic red plaid. Good grief! The thousands of mosquitoes on his back had actually changed the shirt's color! I figured the meaning of "Inowak" should be changed from "The Place Where the River Comes Out" to "The Place Where the Mosquitoes Come Out." That was enough for me. I retraced my steps to the kitchen. Mom's shadow showed through the plastic.

"Come in. Shut the door. Quick!" she exclaimed.

Some pests had hitched a ride on my hat, and she swept them off with her hand.

Thumbing through recipe cards, she said, "The men are getting ready to shuttle kids across the river tomorrow."

Mom knew everything that went on in the camp, probably because the kitchen and meeting hall were the focal points of camp activity. Sometimes, I wondered if she had a high-powered radio antenna in her ever-present hat.

We talked for a while. Even though she had been gone only a few days, she asked how things were back on the homestead. I filled her in as best I could and then inquired about fishing. That is when she provided a noteworthy tidbit.

"Dave shot a young black bear right here in camp, a couple of days ago."

Well, that got my attention. I had never considered this area black bear country.

She continued the tale.

"He dressed it out and staked the carcass in the shallows down the lake aways—to attract pike."

Hmmm. I would investigate the staked-out remains when I got a few minutes. Not now. Not when mosquitoes were at their worst, and not after flying such a distance. I yawned. After a three-hour flight, I had arrived in a different world, and I had not even been on a transatlantic jetliner. The small Piper had transported me from the familiar homestead to a remote lake in the Alaska wilderness.

Mom gave me yet another quick hug. I said goodnight, slipped through the plastic doorway, and headed for my tent.

Around noon the next day, the first load of children arrived, announced by exuberant shouts and laughter, along with footsteps racing up the hill to the camp. Staff members lined the sides of the trail and guided the campers to the main meeting area, where the brown-eyed, raven-haired kids jostled about while a staff member recorded their names and assigned them tents. My only responsibilities were to provide music and to keep track of one tent full of 10-year-old boys at night.

Dave had been flying kids in from the villages all day and showed up just in time for supper with the last load of campers. Everyone was here now, and the staffers herded the youngsters to a row of water-filled wash-basins arranged on a long wooden bench. Bars of soap and towels to dry their hands accompanied the basins. With clean hands, the boys and girls proceeded inside to the awaiting tables. When everyone had gathered, a staffer stood up. A wave of "shushes" spread throughout the room, and the staffer asked God to bless the food. The kids devoured the soup like a plague of locusts, as would be the case at every mealtime. Mom's eyes twinkled in delight to see the kids enjoy the food she had prepared.

Supper wound down. The kitchen helpers tended to the dishes in the kitchen, while the evening program started in the meeting area. After being introduced, I walked to the front, reached behind a mound of boxes, and picked up my guitar. I pulled the pick from between the strings and strummed it once to make sure it was in tune. Satisfied, I told the kids the name of the chorus I would lead. I had chosen 10 songs that I played for my church youth group in Soldotna. The staff provided plenty of support since they knew the words and tunes from their church or childhood camping experiences. Some kids knew the songs from the preceding year and sang with gusto. Some were more interested in my guitar. After I led three choruses, my job was complete, and I walked to the back of the room where I watched a skit by the staff. The campers erupted with gales of laughter and the adults found the performance comical, too.

Then I was ready to escape the commotion and find some quiet. I flipped open my tent door and surveyed the contents. There were now six sleeping bags, more or less on the cots. Some cots had a small bag of personal items beneath them. Cots without such bags usually meant the boy was too poor to have extra clothes or his parent did not bother to help him pack them. I checked for the six-by-six-inch pad of wrinkled tinfoil, which would hold insecticide powder, and found it beneath my cot. Before lights-out, I would ignite it. I was more like a night watchman than an actual counselor and now felt prepared.

A burst of voices let me know the evening program had ended, and I waited outside the tent to see who would show up. I knew only to expect nine- and ten-year-old boys. John, one of the staff, walked up to me with specific information.

"You should have six boys. We put Charlie in with you."

That made me grin. The small boy had a soft voice and a smile like sunshine.

"Okay, great. I'll get a head count before I turn out the lights."

The boys entered by ones and twos, complemented by nonstop chatter.

It was June, and while the sun actually did go down, it never got truly dark, more like dusk. Nevertheless, with the tent flaps closed, it was quite dim inside. I pulled out my flashlight and pointed it between the rows of cots.

"Hey, make sure you use the outhouse before crawling into your sleeping bag," I admonished.

Two of the lads made a beeline for the door. The rest sat on the edges of their cots, removed their shoes, and snuggled into their sleeping bags. Except for Charlie. Charlie came over and took my hand with both of his. Then he looked up at me.

"Mr. Mark? Can I sleep on the bed next to yours?" he asked wistfully.

"Whose bag is there now?" I asked, keeping my tone neutral.

Charlie clung to my hand and scowled. He shook his head to indicate it was one of the boys who had just left, "That's Ivan's. But he doesn't know you."

I thought about it briefly, then permitted him to swap cots. I would deal with any fallout when the owner of the displaced sleeping bag returned.

Meanwhile, a staff member popped in with a yellow cardboard can containing tan-colored powder.

"You need some?" He asked.

"Sure do, thank you," I replied.

I slid the square of tinfoil out from under my cot and he sprinkled a two-inch-high cone of the powder on its shiny surface. With a bob of his head, the staffer departed for the next tent.

I pulled out a book of matches, ran one across the striker, and held the lit match to the powder. A spiral of smoke appeared. Satisfied that the insecticide would continue to smolder, I blew out the match. In theory, the substance would keep the mosquitoes out and kill any buzzing around in the tent. In theory.

The two boys returned. Ivan saw Charlie staring up at him from what had once been his cot.

"Hey, what are you doing? That's my bed," Ivan demanded.

Charlie was not a big fellow by any stretch of the imagination, but he was not intimidated.

"Yours is over there now," he said assertively.

Charlie pointed to a different cot. Ivan shrugged, clomped over to his reassigned bed, kicked his shoes off, and crawled into his sleeping bag. I had watched similar interactions before. There was a pecking order within villages and often between villages, usually set by a family's status. Regardless, just because Charlie was my friend did not mean I would play favorites.

The boys were all accounted for, so I called for their attention.

"Okay, boys. I'm going to pray before we go to sleep."

The tent grew quiet.

"Dear Lord, thank you for bringing these boys safely to camp. Give us a good night of rest. In Jesus' name, amen."

"Everybody ready for lights-out?" I asked.

There was a chorus of yeses, although it may not have been unanimous.

I switched the flashlight off, and the tent plunged into darkness. I lay in my sleeping bag and listened to the whispers, which over time became fewer and fewer. The occasional drone of a mosquito told me I would probably donate blood to one of the suckers during the night. It had been a long day, and I soon fell asleep, awakened at one point by a faint whimper. After a moment, I heard a child's voice consoling the anxious camper, and it was once again quiet.

The next morning, I figured out the week's routine. Meals were interspersed with outdoor activities, indoor arts and crafts, and Bible stories on a flannel graph board. I needed to be around only during the evening, so I filled my day with other things. Sometimes I got creative, such as when I discovered horseflies annoying Mom in the kitchen. They droned around camp, and some got trapped inside the kitchen. The flies buzzed and bumped along the plastic until they got tired, at which point, they crawled until they caught their breath or whatever flies did when they needed a break.

I thought of my old U-control model airplanes and had an idea. Those gas-powered airplanes flew in a circle, tethered to a person in the middle by 20 feet of strong string. The concept was simple. Previously, a buddy had started the model's engine and released it, while I stood in the middle and guided the plane around in a circle. After a few quick revolutions, I either lost control of the airplane or got dizzy and fell down. Either way, the flight ended with a broken airplane tangled up in string, and me lying in the dirt wondering why people thought that was fun.

What if I could capture a horsefly and fly it like a model airplane? I found a piece of thread in one of the craft boxes and tore off six feet. Then I went back to the kitchen to round up a horsefly. They were not hard to catch. Soon I had one on its back on the countertop. Mom watched as I worked to capture one of its six legs.

"Hold still, varmint!" I muttered.

I finally managed to wrangle the critter into submission and lasso one of the legs with a loop of thread. I tied a knot and turned the fly loose. It buzzed off and I fed it some string. Oh, this was fun! Of course, Mom did not want my latest flying experiment in the kitchen and sent me outside.

I dragged the struggling fly with me, where it flew around on the end of my string. Naturally, I attracted attention with my hand held high above

223

my head, flaunting my invisible miniature airplane. More than once, I was asked, "What on earth are you doing, Mark?"

"I'm flying a fly," I said, pointing upward where the fly winged back and forth.

When the questioners spotted the fly, they started laughing. Unsurprisingly, Charlie wanted to follow me everywhere and try his hand at fly-flying.

The horseflies were strong fliers but had issues similar to real airplanes. I discovered that if I tied the string around a rear leg, and turned the fly loose, it would fly straight up and out of sight, the string zigzagging crazily behind it. Its center of gravity was too far back for level flight, just like in a real airplane loaded too far back.

Sometimes when I had a free moment, I would take one of the boats out on the lake and fish for Northern pike. On this trip, I had brought a sturdy rod and lures I knew pike liked. My first year at Inowak, I had not brought fishing gear, so I had to improvise. Dave Penz had dug out a reel, a steel leader, and a treble hook for me to use. I'd found a stick to serve as a pole and attached the reel to it with wire. I twisted the wire tight with a pair of pliers and covered the sharp ends of the wire with duct tape. At the rod's tip, I made a guide from another loop of wire, held in place by a small nail. With the fishing rod completed, I went to work on a lure. I had no idea what I was doing, but I had seen pictures of plugs used to catch bass.

While there were no bass within several thousand miles of this place, I figured I would make a plug anyway. I had no way to make a spinner or spoon, which were lures Northern pike would chase. I whittled the plug body to about the size of the small voles that ran in the grass around the camp. I even used a felt-tip marker to put eyes on it, so the fish would know which end was which. The treble hook was anchored to the body with a small, bent-over finishing nail. The hook did not pivot, but it was the best I could do.

Later in the day, I got permission to take one of the boats out and I motored to a spot across from the camp. I tried a couple of casts with my makeshift rod. It was pathetic. Fifteen feet was about all the farther I could get the plug to go. It was too light, and I had no weights to add. Also, the wooden plug just bobbed and wobbled on the surface when I reeled it in. After a few more futile casts, I powered to a different spot and tried again.

Some disappointing casts later, there was a sudden swirl in the reeds, and my plug disappeared with a splash! I felt the weight of the fish on the line and hoped the line would hold. I had no idea how strong the line was, or whether my cockeyed rod would hold together. The fish lunged under the boat, then back into the reeds. I caught a glimpse of a torpedo shape and knew I had a large Northern, way too big for my makeshift fishing gear.

I felt a surge of adrenaline. Would my makeshift line break? Finally, the fish tired and I brought it close to the boat. Now what? I did not have a net, and I did not trust the line, or even the hook to hold the weight of the fish if I pulled it over the side of the boat. I knew better than to get my fingers close to the mouth full of razor-sharp teeth. Eventually, I managed to get a couple of fingers behind the gill cover and drag it over the side. I whooped! It was the biggest pike I had ever caught! It lay on the bottom of the boat and glared at me with baleful eyes. Ha! I headed back to the dock, parked the boat, and hurried up the bank with my prize. Outside the kitchen, I beckoned Mom.

"Mom! Mom! Look what I caught!" I yelled.

She poked her head out to see what caused my elation. My yells had attracted other adults and campers, and a small crowd collected around me. Mom sized up the fish.

"Oh, that's a nice one! I think we can use it," she said. "Smaller pike have so many fine bones and are such a chore to prepare."

Someone found a measuring tape. The pike stretched 34 inches.

Mom cooked the fish. I boiled the flesh off the lower jaw and kept the toothy reminder in a drawer in my bedroom with my other treasures. The largest teeth measured over one-half inches long.

Despite the mosquitoes, the campers loved to play in the water, and activities were planned to accommodate that interest. Up the lake, past the camp, the water became shallow. It was slowly filling with dead vegetation, and I suspected a few billion dead mosquitoes, too. Some years, the staff placed a 30-by-30-foot heavy-duty tarp in a muddy depression along the shore, and let it fill with water. The sun heated the water and made it a pleasant, safe place for the kids to swim, or at least splash around. These kids had lived around water their entire lives, but tepid lake water was a rare treat.

There was also a pair of "Jesus shoes," which the more daring used to walk on water. The shoes were simply large blocks of Styrofoam with slots for feet. Kids who managed to walk a few steps invariably ended up like Peter, on the Sea of Galilee in the Bible story, and they floundered. I'm sure a Bible lesson was ready to be taught from their experiences.

One day I stopped by the kitchen to visit with Mom, who was stirring up a batch of oatmeal cookies.

"Hi, Mom. Can I help you with something?" I asked, eyeing the dough.

I thought maybe I could lick the spoon when she was finished. Unfortunately, this was not the case.

"Hi Mark. Why don't you see if you can help Dave? He's down by the creek fixing the water pump. It quit yesterday, and our water is getting low."

She was referring to replenishing water barrels by the kitchen.

"Oh, okay," I replied.

I left the kitchen and rambled off to find Dave. Not difficult. I merely followed the one-inch black plastic tubing from the barrels, across the camp, and down through the birch trees to the creek. There he was, stooped over the misbehaving pump. He heard my footsteps and glanced up briefly.

"Can I give you a hand?" I asked. "What happened?"

Oily grime covered his hands, and he held up a broken metal circle.

"The head gasket is shot," he stated, then sighed.

I was thinking this was a disaster. There were no hardware stores down the street, and I doubted the general store in Sleetmute, or even McGrath, would have that specific gasket. The most likely place to find one was Anchorage. To obtain one, would mean the loss of a day, not to mention 40 gallons of aviation fuel to fly there and back.

"Mark, can you go get a medium-sized tin can from your mom?" He asked. "I'll go get some snips."

I ran back to the kitchen and relayed the request.

Mom sorted through an assortment of empty tins and handed me one.

"Thanks, Mom," I told her and clawed back through the plastic draping the doorway.

Back at the creek, I handed Dave the can and watched him craft a new gasket. He cut the can open and flattened it against a block of wood. Then using the old gasket as a template, he traced the shape with a nail. I observed in rapt attention. He proceeded to cut along the etched lines with the metal snips. Next, he set the new gasket on the cylinder and precisely marked where the head bolts would be. After trimming those areas, the gasket was completed. He put the crafted piece on the cylinder, placed the cylinder head on top, and started the head bolts. All the pieces were now in place, and he squinted closely at the edges, to be sure the gasket was centered. Satisfied, he tightened the head bolts, straightened up, pulled a rag from his jacket pocket, and wiped his oily hands.

"Well, what do you think?" he asked.

"Wow! Looks good to me!" My admiration was evident.

He smiled. "Let's see if it works."

He grabbed the starter rope, set the choke, and pulled the engine through a couple of times, but it did not fire.

"It's got compression," he stated.

No doubt he could tell by the resistance when he pulled the starter rope. He adjusted the throttle and again tugged the rope. After a few more pulls, the engine sputtered and ran.

For me, this was a near miracle; for Dave Penz, it was just another day in the boonies.

One evening, Mom prepared a roast from a small black bear that had wandered into camp. Despite my doubts, the meat was delicious. I should have known Mom's uncanny ability to tame wild game for the table would yield a culinary delight. Of course, a young black bear was one thing. A chunk of grizzly meat was another. Years before, Dad had brought home a piece of greasy grizzly, and she had sent him right back out the door.

"It stinks!" she had said. And that was the end of that.

The black bear feast reminded me of the carcass staked out in the lake and I decided to pay it a visit. I had gotten permission earlier to take one of the boats down the lake, and after I was through leading choruses, I picked up my fishing pole and made my way down to the dock. Yes, the mosquitoes were awful, but once I was underway, I left them behind. A few minutes later, I located the carcass and throttled back to an idle.

The stake used to anchor the remains was visible, as was the top of the rib cage. I guessed the clear water was about three or four feet deep there.

I shut down the motor and let the boat drift to a stop, about 30 to 40 feet from the stake. The surface of the water was glassy-calm. I selected a #3 Mepps' spinner, snapped it on the steel leader, and made my first cast. As soon as the lure splashed down, I saw a pair of V-shaped ripples disturb the water next to the carcass. The only fish in this lake that would leave a trail like that were pike. And a pair of them were headed for the spinner.

I laughed quietly. This was my kind of fishing. I could not see the fish, but I knew where they were by watching the wake they left. I kept retrieving and watching the V's close in. One darted ahead of the other and the tip of my rod sagged when the fish struck. It fought for a while, but soon I had the toothy fish next to the boat. Rod in one hand, I reached over the side with a pair of needle-nose pliers in the other and removed the hook from the throat of the struggling fish. It was well over two feet long, but I released it. The camp was sufficiently stocked with salmon, taken from the Kuskokwim, and did not need a bony pike.

I made another cast and was rewarded with yet another good-sized Northern. Eventually, the pike-bite dropped off, and I headed back to camp. When I related my experience to some of the other guys, they told me the larger pike was feeding on the carcass and aggressively chased smaller fish away. Whatever the reason, it made for fun fishing.

The volunteers could catch their breath during the day or two between the week-long camps, when they had time to themselves without focusing on the emotional and physical needs of children. Mom could find a few minutes to read a book and write letters. Sometimes, Dave flew out to get supplies or to swap out staff. For those of us who stayed in camp, it was Bath Day. After a week of woodsmoke, bug repellent, and sweat, it was a welcome reprieve, if not for me, for those in my proximity. The downside was that the layers of smoke and bug spray had developed an aromatic halo around me, which even mosquitoes hesitated to penetrate. It would now all be washed away and I would have to start the process over again. The bathhouse was in a green canvas tent, next to the supply tent. Inside, on the canvas floor, was a plastic-lined wooden trough, approximately 24 inches wide, 48 inches long, and 11 inches deep.

On bath day, water was heated in the kitchen and carried over in metal buckets. Between patrons, the trough was emptied and resupplied. A handwritten "Occupied" sign pinned to the door flap indicated the need for privacy. One time, in the subdued light, I was scared half to death by what I thought was a crazy man in the tent with me! As it turned out, it was only my reflection in the mirror hanging on the tent pole. I then realized keeping my wild, curly hair concealed beneath my hat was essential during waking hours. As rustic as it was, we appreciated this simple indulgence in the middle of nowhere and looked forward to Bath Day.

Weekends were also a time when Mom and I could talk uninterrupted.

"I'm concerned about that really small girl," Mom confided. "She's so quiet and the other children seem to avoid her." Mom laid down her pencil from a note she was writing and sighed. I didn't know what to say and remained quiet. Mom continued for a bit, then mentioned a staff member who was overwhelmed by the heart-breaking situations some of the children came from in the villages. She also revealed how the rugged conditions of the camp were hard on some of the staff.

This talk was not gossip. I recognized the burden she carried was out of genuine concern and what she said never went beyond me.

After a while, she paused and looked me square in the eye. "What about you? What are your concerns?"

That made me mentally squirm because I thought my questions were not all *that* important, except perhaps to me. But since I never felt judged by her, I felt free to lay out some of my thoughts. I was older now and my inquiries were no longer about asking permission to ride my bike somewhere. My world had grown and so had my list of questions. Should I go to college? If so, how did I decide what to study? So many fields and topics were interesting to me. Would I have to leave Alaska? How did my musical ability fit in? And why was talking to girls I liked so scary? She listened intently and offered tender words of wisdom, mother to her son.

Then, she reached for my arm, "Oh, Mark. I pray for you. Keep asking God for guidance. He will direct you. Whatever you choose, use your abilities and talents for Him."

She paused briefly then concluded with, "You know your dad and I love you no matter what you decide."

Her nurturing attitude helped me feel anchored, even when I did not understand my own internal turmoil. Often, I left these visits with a cookie, a gentle reminder that no matter how old I got to be, I would always be her little boy.

My two weeks were suddenly over, and I was shuttled back to the PA-12 on the gravel bar. I had no passengers for the flight back. Mom and Jan were scheduled to stay an additional week and would fly back with one of the missionary pilots. I loaded my few belongings into the baggage compartment, next to the now empty fuel cans and funnel, and mentally shifted gears from guitar player/boat driver/night watchman to pilot. After completing the preflight inspection, I climbed aboard and fired up the Lycoming. Before long, I was back in the air. I circled over the camp. The boat that had dropped me at the plane was already back on the lake, trailed by a frothy wake. A bit of smoke marked the kitchen tent where Mom undoubtedly was preparing lunch.

At 18, I was now the pilot, alone in Dad's airplane, doing what I had dreamed about since I had toddled to his J-3 on the banks of the Yukon River. I rolled out on an easterly heading and continued to climb toward the mountains, too far away to see, but beyond which lay home. After a while, I reached over and found the oatmeal cookies Mom had sent along with me.

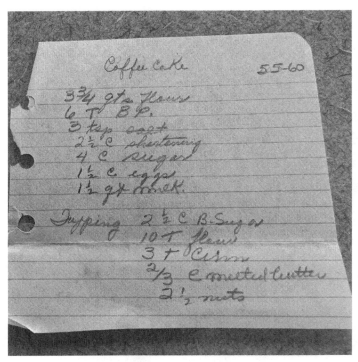

Camp Inowak Cinnamon Coffee Cake

Typical Camp Menus

Breakfast—pancakes and hot chocolate.

Lunch—pilot bread, peanut butter, Jello or canned fruit for dessert.

*Supper—baked fish, hash brown potatoes made
from dehydrated potatoes, canned peas, apple crisp
for dessert (made from dehydrated apples).*

WHAT BROUGHT DAVE PENZ TO ALASKA?

How did his passion to serve the Native people develop? In "Living Gold: The Story of Dave and Vera Penz of Kako, Alaska," read about Dave Penz, his family, Camp Inowak, and other Christian ministries that Dave poured his heart and energy into. No matter the adversity, this indomitable man never slowed down.

CHAPTER 14

BLOWN AWAY

"I'M GOING TO BE LATE," I muttered.

It was a typical late February workday morning in 1987. The dim, pre-dawn sky offered little clue as to the day's weather. While I spread peanut butter on sandwich bread, I glanced at my watch. It read 7:30 a.m.

At age 31 I had earned a two-year degree in Industrial Electronics and worked north of Kenai at Dresser Atlas, an international oilfield service company. I was married now, too, to Patti Kvalvik, whose family had come to Soldotna the same year we had, in 1961. They lived along the Kenai River, and while I played in the creek and gravel pits, Patti and her siblings caught salmon only two miles away. We finally met when Patti joined our church youth group. The Gaede-80 Homestead remained my home, and we lived on a piece of acreage along the airstrip, where I had built a house.

Another milestone was that after high school, I no longer considered myself "short." I'd finally grown to 5 feet, 10 inches, Dad's height.

Grabbing my lunch bag, I hurried to the enclosed back porch where my boots, coats, and other outdoor gear were stored. Alaskans call this area between the door into the house and the door from the outdoors, an "arctic entry." It keeps the frigid air outside where it belongs. I wormed my way into my black snowsuit, then added a wool hat and heavy gloves. Snugging the snowsuit collar tighter around my neck, I left the house and plodded down the snowy path to the J-3, which was parked conveniently on the edge of the runway, 100 feet from my house. Yes, the orange J-3 Cub Dad had flown was mine now.

Although I could drive to my place of work, I had been saving time by flying. The 20-mile flight shaved 10 minutes off the commute, and I avoided traffic on icy roads. Besides, I preferred flying to driving. I followed the Cook Inlet coast the entire way. A lake downhill from the shop provided a handy place to land and take off.

Again, I glanced overhead. Thin strands of high clouds dominated the sky. The windsock, perched in a tall tree across the runway, moved slightly with a light northerly breeze. This observation was the extent of my weather briefing.

Even though I was tardy getting out the door, no extra time would be spent getting the airplane into the air. Cloud cover overnight had kept frost from forming on the J-3's wings, and though below freezing, I did not have to preheat the engine. It was ready and waiting. Warm weather had settled the snow to 12 to 15 inches, which made it easy to circle the airplane for my preflight. After untying the ropes that secured each wing, I lifted each ski and removed the block of wood I had placed there after the previous flight to prevent the skis from bonding to the snow.

I went through the routine to manually start the engine and soon had it running. I skirted the spinning propellor, and with my shoulders hunched against the prop blast, hurried to the plane's side door. The cross bars over the instrument panel provided a handhold, and I hoisted myself into the narrow cabin. A quick scan of the few gauges said all was well. I fastened my safety harness and positioned my hearing protectors. When I opened the throttle, the J-3 slid easily from its parking spot. After years of fighting with skis stuck to the snow, the addition of Teflon bottoms made a significant difference in reducing friction. In some cases, the skis were too slick, and like huskies lunging in their traces, the plane wanted to move immediately, making the usual pre-takeoff RPM check awkward. After completing the checklist, I advanced the throttle smoothly and was airborne after a short 100 feet. I loved how the Cub eagerly jumped into the air as if it disdained being earthbound.

I avoided the busy controlled airspace over the Kenai airport and kept the airplane nose pointed upwards until I reached the uncontrolled airspace of 3,000 feet.

Although heavily filtered by the clouds, daylight increased as the sun rose higher. I noticed the visibility was unlimited in most directions, restricted only by the ranges of mountains to the east and west, and the curvature of the earth to the north and south. Since I could see the tops of the volcanoes 40 miles to the west, I knew the clouds were at least 11,000 feet above the ground. I always watched the weather closely since I did not want to risk getting stranded at work if it turned bad.

Steam from the refinery not far from my workplace indicated a steady north wind. I set up my approach to my landing site. The lake, surrounded by low, spruce-covered hills, was well over a mile long, and even though the hills caused some turbulence when the wind blew across them, they had numerous coves with protection. The J-3 was not designed with flaps, so once I cleared the hill on the south end, I put the airplane into a slip, which increased the angle and rate of descent without increasing the speed of the aircraft; basically, flying the aircraft sideways and downward.

As the snowy surface of the lake rose to meet me, I straightened the airplane, touched down on the crusty snow, and taxied to my customary spot, 100 yards from the shop. I felt confident the plane was secure in this location and never tied it down. I did, however, grab two wooden two-by-four blocks from the baggage compartment and place them beneath the skis.

Leaving the plane, I hiked up the lightly packed snow machine trail to the shop. Along the way, I noticed the tops of spruce trees moving slightly in the breeze. The North Kenai area jutted into Cook Inlet and subsequently experienced more wind. For instance, the wind could be blowing 15 to 25 mph at work, while at home the leaves would be barely moving. A breeze here at work didn't concern me, and without a second thought, I walked into the shop.

After a quick greeting to the other employees at work, I started my daily routine of repairing and calibrating electronic equipment, all the while half-listening to an AM radio in the lab.

By 10 a.m., the wind had increased considerably. I could see the 60- to-80-foot spruce trees start to dance outside the window.

At 11:30 a.m., the radio station issued a warning from the FAA, urging pilots to check their airplanes and make sure they were secured. The wind was now strong enough to break the crusty snow loose and send it swirling. It was high time I checked my J-3.

When I reached the airplane, I estimated the gusts were at 30 mph. Nevertheless, the plane only rocked slightly when a stronger gust passed. To position the airplane more squarely into the wind, I temporarily removed the blocks under the skis, lifted the tail, and turned it slightly. Before leaving the aircraft, I secured the control stick tightly with the seatbelt, which would prevent the control surfaces from fluttering in the wind and wearing out the hinge pins on the ailerons or rudder.

Shortly after lunch, Patti called. "It's really stormy here. Are you sure you want to fly home in this wind?"

I could hear the apprehension in her voice. Once again, I scanned the view outside my window. Yes, it was windy here, but I was sure it would not be as bad at home. I kept my voice cheerful and confident.

"Oh, I don't think it will be a problem," I responded. "See you in a few hours."

At 3 p.m., the power at the shop went down. Work ended. The group of us at the shop clustered at a window and talked about how badly the trees whipped around. We speculated they were falling on the powerlines causing the lines to short out. We were correct.

By 4 p.m., it was apparent the power would not be coming back on anytime soon. Our boss told us to go home. I tugged on my snowsuit, waved goodbye to my work buddies, and headed to the lake.

Unknown to me, an unusually powerful storm had moved into the Gulf of Alaska, and the pressure gradient between that low pressure and the high pressure that sat anchored in the middle of the state was quite steep. This was manifested as a massive river of wind. In this case, it was funneling down Cook Inlet. In my 27 years of flying on the Kenai Peninsula, I had never observed wind of this intensity in the Kenai/Soldotna area. I was yet to comprehend the magnitude of this occurrence. Therefore, I was still unconcerned. I fired up the J-3 and climbed in.

When the power went down, the office telephones died. Little did I know that Dad had desperately tried to warn me against flying home. When he could not reach me by phone, he jumped into his car and headed to my shop, a 30-minute drive from his clinic in Soldotna. As I started my takeoff run, Dad was standing on the hill behind me, watching his only son depart into a maelstrom with a lightweight J-3.

"Takeoff run," in this case, was a misnomer. When I increased the RPM to takeoff power, I was immediately airborne, even though I had not traveled more than a dozen feet. Turbulence immediately hit. As I climbed through the critical first few hundred feet, I was fully occupied with keeping the wings level. At 500 feet, the air smoothed out and I continued up to 3,000 feet. Although the plane was steady at this altitude, I could tell there was tremendous wind. It was the wind correction angle that gave me the clue. To fly a straight track over the shoreline below, I had to point the nose of the J-3 about 30 degrees inland. In other words, I was crabbing or flying sideways. With a quartering tailwind, I was making an unusually swift return flight.

It was not until I passed over Kenai that I started to feel uneasy. On most days,

numerous small planes flew in and out of the Kenai Airport. Since the J-3 had no electrical system and no radio, I could not monitor air traffic in that way. I was startled to realize that not a single airplane was anywhere in sight. What I did see were trees rippling back and forth like a field of hay in the wind. This was from 3,000 feet up. I had never witnessed anything like this before.

I started my descent. By the time I reached the homestead, I was already considering landing alternatives. While a generous half mile long, the homestead strip appears quite narrow since it is carved out of the forest and is bordered by 60-foot spruce. I passed over the strip at 2,000 feet, made a 180-degree turn, and set up my approach, less than a half mile out. I was still just under 2,000 feet. On any other day, at this point, I would have been at 500 feet. Even though it had been a smooth flight thus far, I was leery of turbulence lurking closer to the ground. My entire body tensed as I felt my way downward.

When the airplane descended through 1,500 feet, it began to jiggle and shudder.

The trees below whipped back and forth. I had been wholly focused on my approach and keeping that point ahead in view, so when I glanced to the side, at the road that paralleled my approach, I was shocked to see I had advanced only a few hundred feet toward the landing strip. I checked my airspeed. It read 75 mph. My normal approach speed was 50 mph. If

I had throttled back to 50 mph, I would have been motionless above the ground, or maybe even going backwards. The implications made my head spin. I was flying in winds close to 70 mph, well outside the parameters the J-3 was designed for wind-wise.

As if that was not unnerving enough, the wind was blowing across the runway at an angle, and I could see snow spiraling down it. It looked like a horizontal tornado. Just like my father before me, I was processing information and making decisions. I knew that attempting to land on our strip was a guaranteed disaster.

When I advanced the throttle and pulled the stick back slightly to abort my approach, my altitude was still 1,200 feet. As I turned away to the east, my peripheral vision picked up a moving vehicle on the road at the end of the strip. I spared a glance and recognized the truck belonged to Roger Rupp, my sister Ruth's husband. Roger was also a pilot, and I felt some relief knowing he had seen my predicament.

At warp speed, my mind sorted through the options for landing. With a cruise speed of 82 mph into a headwind of 70 mph, my choices were limited. Added to my alarm, the fuel bobber in the nose tank had just bottomed out. I had approximately 30 minutes of flight time remaining. Accordingly, Kenai, only 10 miles to the north, was out of range. The Soldotna airport was only three miles to the east, but that runway was laid out in an east-west direction. I quickly ruled out landing there in a near-hurricane crosswind. That left lakes, swamps, roads, and open fields.

A half mile east of the homestead, down Echo Lake Road, there were several snow-covered hayfields. I figured one of those might work for an emergency landing. I chose the field closest to the road and began my approach. My ground speed was ridiculously slow, and instead of reducing the engine speed to idle, like I customarily did when landing, I had to keep the engine running faster to prevent the plane from drifting backward.

Although the field was about 500 feet long, an adequate distance to land in a typical situation, that really did not matter. In the wind, I would be essentially landing like a helicopter, hovering over one spot and adjusting the throttle to let the airplane inch downward.

The gusts kept me busy at the controls as the wings rocked and the J-3 rose and fell with the changing currents. When I touched down on the crusty snow, I pulled back the throttle. Instead of stopping, the airplane slid backward! My adrenaline, which had already risen to a high pitch now spiked even higher. At any moment, the back of the skis could catch and pitch the plane on its back. Even though I no longer perceived myself to be in a life-threatening situation, I was concerned that the wind might destroy the airplane.

I gripped the stick with white knuckles, pushed it forward, and the tail popped off the ground. When I added a bit of power to stop the rearward slide, the J-3 became airborne again. I gently maneuvered it back onto the snow. I had to keep the engine running to prevent the aircraft from flying or sliding backward, but if I tried to taxi, the airplane became airborne. In a normal situation, I would have simply pushed the nose downward, to keep the plane on the ground. This was not a normal situation. With that much wind blowing over the wings and control surfaces, the plane would either flip on its back or nose over.

There I sat. Fuel running out. Constantly working the control stick to keep the airplane upright and on the snow. I figured I was minutes away from hearing the engine sputter, at which point the game was up, and the J-3 would be crumpled like old newsprint ready to start a fire.

Suddenly, out of the corner of my eye, I spied figures making their way across the field in my direction. I recognized Roger. When he had seen me abort my landing on the homestead strip, he hastily rounded up his kids and my dad and headed out to search for me. He and Dad figured I would pick a spot like this, and in under 15 minutes, they were on the scene to assist me. Needless to say, I was overjoyed to see familiar people; people who understood flying.

I motioned for them to grab both wings. Dad and Roger's oldest son caught hold of the left wing. Then Roger and his daughter seized the other one. I added power and slowly started sliding forward toward the end of the field, bordered by a fence, beyond which stood a dense stand of 20-foot-high spruce. If I could get close enough, the spruce would cut the wind. We were making good, but slow, progress, and I started to breathe easier, not that I was relaxed or had let down my guard.

Unexpectedly, a gust lifted the right wing, yanking Roger and his daughter off the ground! I fought with the wind to keep the plane level. His daughter lost her grip and fell onto the snow. Roger hung on for dear life. The gust passed and the wings leveled. I could feel the skis were back on the ground. Slowly, we continued our struggling march down the field.

Once there, I let out a deep breath and switched the engine off. Sheltered by the trees, the wings no longer rocked, although I could still hear the wind whistling through the branches. I undid my seatbelt and climbed out.

"Boy, you sure had us scared!" said Dad. This emotion came from my father, who never registered fear with his own near-death flying experiences.

"I scared myself," I said. After gripping the stick so tightly, I clenched and unclenched my hand to get the stiffness out.

"I was sure glad to see you abort landing on the homestead strip," added Roger. His voice was matter-of-fact, but concern showed in his eyes.

He continued. "The wind has been snapping tie-down ropes off planes on Gaede Private Airstrip. Kraxbergers even brought over one of their big rigs to tie Scott and Rick's plane to."

I stuck my head back in the J-3, rummaged around in the back, and pulled out tie-down ropes. As Roger, Dad, and I worked to secure the airplane to the fence, I glanced over at Roger's daughter.

"I see you went flying," I teased.

She laughed. "Yes, I kind of did, didn't I."

"Thanks for helping. I don't know what would have happened without you guys."

The others headed back toward the vehicles parked on the road, while I made one more check of the ropes. This J-3 was my airplane and my responsibility. Dad had taught me well. The fact that he did not double-check the ropes told me he thought so, too.

Satisfied the J-3 could now weather the rest of the storm, I hurried to catch up with my homestead family. Roger and his two children departed in his pickup, and I slid in next to Dad in his car. As we drove off, I looked back at the J-3 and thought it looked so small and forlorn, tied up to the fence like a lost pony.

As it turned out, it was three days before the wind died down enough to bring the J-3 back to its familiar pasture.

CHAPTER 15

FULL CIRCLE

AFTER A 35-YEAR CAREER in the oil industry and oftentimes abroad, my family and I returned to the Gaede homestead in 2014. Mom and Dad had long since taken up residence in their heavenly home and turned the keys of their earthly habitation over to their kids. The four of us, Naomi, Ruth, Mishal, and I, had determined to keep the homestead intact rather than sell it.

More than 50 years after Mom and Dad "proved up" the Gaede 80-acre homestead, a drive down the now-paved Gas Well Road yields a study in contrasts. At the corner of Gas Well and Kalifonsky Beach Road, Jackson's field is still planted and harvested by the next generation; yet, just beyond the fields, the woods have been cut down to build a subdivision. The gravel pits by Slikok Creek, which we neighborhood kids spent so many summer days exploring, were at some point deemed dangerous and filled and leveled. The creek still runs under the road, but kids no longer splash or catch frogs there. Evidence of the Echo Lake forest fire, which burned so close to our homestead, has disappeared, covered by the regrowth of aspen and spruce.

A majority of the homesteads like ours, established in the early 1960s, did not last beyond the second generation. Maintaining acreage is hard work, and some inheritors could not afford the time, energy, or money to keep up the property. Others had no interest in the land. Whatever the reasons, the properties were sold off. Fortunately for us, our immediate neighbors, the Herrs and Kraxbergers, kept their property in the family, as did we. These adjacent blocks of land now appear as an island surrounded by subdivisions and commercial development.

A turn off of Gas Well onto the road in front of the homestead house, now called Gaede Lane, is a step back in time. We allowed the trees along the road to grow back, and they now hug the road as they did before our parents cleared them, in 1962. On the left is a log cabin. The original cabin burned in 2005, although we salvaged one bedroom, and with nostalgia and loving care, we turned it into a mini-cabin. My sister, Naomi, built another cabin in the same spot. Directly across the road from the cabin is an A-frame, built in the early 1970s with the help of Grandma and Grandpa Leppke. A little farther down the road is the circle drive leading to the original homestead house.

When my wife, Patti, and I moved back, the house was in serious disrepair. Rather than bulldoze it under as some people suggested, we decided to rebuild it. The process took two years, with Patti, our daughter, Kenya, and I doing most of the work. We stripped out everything: plumbing, electrical, insulation, and windows and doors. Then, we stored materials that could be repurposed in an old hangar.

The bones of the house proved to be solid. With the exception of an expanded front porch, the footprint of the house remained the same. I furred out the two-by-four-foot studded walls to accommodate more insulation and installed insulated windows. Next came modernized wiring and plumbing, along with an efficient fireplace in place of a wood stove.

As I worked to rebuild the homestead, I realized how much I was reliving my childhood and had become like my dad. In the same way, my parents and us children had relied on the cabin when the house was first built, my own family and I lived in the cabin while rebuilding the homestead house.

Then, a few years after completing the house, I built a hangar on the original 60-by-32-foot concrete slab. We siblings had torn down the old hangar years before when the homemade trusses began to splinter under the weight of winter snow.

I rebuilt the old chicken coop, reusing as much of the vintage material as possible. I turned the weathered siding around, so the exterior looked like new again.

When the barn listed badly and became unsound, it was torn down.

The woodshed, built from untreated spruce logs and slab siding, had rotted, settled, and finally came to rest on the top of an old unused freezer. All this needed to be tidied up.

At times, these renovations were like an archaeological dig. Alongside the hangar, under a half-dozen decaying tires, were 12-volt batteries. Farther down, I discovered a bent propeller, evidence of yet another one of Dad's "learning experiences." Added to the historical reminders were coils of wire, half-rotted rough-cut timbers, pieces of iron pipe, and even one of my childhood bicycle frames.

In addition to dealing with the buildings, the land needed attention. Nature eagerly reclaimed the disturbed ground. The grass runway, once fertilized and harvested annually, had been left unattended for almost 20 years. Although used by Roger for his aircraft repair business, spruce and aspen trees ventured out into the sunlight of the airstrip and thrived there.

As my father had done many years earlier, I purchased a small tractor in 2020 to help with the many homestead chores. Instead of his gray and red Ford tractor, a PTO-driven brush hog on my green John Deere beats back the willows and smaller trees on the taxiways and runway, while my chainsaw deals with the larger ones. Kenya inherited some of the homestead spirit and is eager to fell trees and drive a tractor, too.

Every year, I battle an invasive plant species. Spruce bark beetles have returned to decimate the tall, mature spruce trees, and the dry, gray skeletal trees are a forest fire waiting to happen. Homesteading is back-breaking work; nonetheless, from summer through fall, I cut down these trees, strip the branches, and cut the logs into firewood. Following our parents' example, in the early winter, when the ground is protected by snow, our remaining homestead family assembles at the end of the airstrip for the annual burning of mounds of branches.

During a recent summer, I brought in a portable mill to cut selected logs into rough-cut lumber, not unlike what Dad did when he and Mom carved the runway in the forest.

The homestead is filled with memories. Some are tangible. The cabin Naomi built serves as a repository for family memorabilia. In the basement, old snowshoes, Dad's spark-burned green army surplus jacket, wooden Blazo boxes, the pump organ, two accordions, two mandolins, and Dad's medical bag reside as does the rug mount of my first mountain goat. I built a low table from an original woodshed door and added that to the collection. Upstairs, Mom's moose head hangs on the wall, along with another of my Dall sheep mounts.

Back at the homestead house, a new woodshed stands where the first one stood. The old outhouse, however, remains buried, overgrown with moss and lowbush cranberries. Inside the front entry of the house, my Dall sheep from the Port Alsworth hunt is displayed, as well as a trophy-class mountain goat I shot many years later on the same mountain Dad slid off when I was 14.

Downstairs, the room that was once my bedroom now serves as an office and music production room. As a teenager, I used to sit on my bed, strum my guitar, and wonder what it would be like to write and record music in a professional studio. Now, in that same room, I have the ability to record unlimited high-quality digital soundtracks and have access to terabytes of professional sound libraries with tens of thousands of sounds at my fingertips. Not only that, with a keystroke on my computer, I can send a completed composition to my YouTube channel and reach nearly anyone in the world. I am limited only by my imagination and the hours in a day. Some days, I work on original music, other days I prepare for a Sunday church service. Whatever the reason, scarcely a day goes by when I am not working on some musical project. All this, from what had been my boyhood "bunker."

Dad took hundreds of pictures and movies. I, too, enjoy taking pictures, which has become so much easier with the advent of digital photography. Later in his life, Dad spent hundreds of thousands of dollars funding and producing movies. I use a smartphone, compose my own musical scores, and post them to my YouTube channel.

I still fly. I inherited Dad's final airplane, a Piper PA-18 Super Cub. Like most things on the homestead, it was due for some work, and I hired Roger to rebuild it. Just like the house, we stripped it down to the bare frame, and it was an opportunity to address the issues that irritated me when I flew with Dad. The standard 18-gallon fuel tanks were replaced with 30-gallon units, which gave me a range of over seven-and-a-half hour's flight time. Five-gallon cans with a funnel and smelly chamois filter are history. With a radio and an intercom, it is now possible to carry on a conversation with my passenger while in the air. And the seats have more padding.

Our daughter flies with me. One of our favorite outings is to Mount Augustine. The waters of Cook Inlet are still cold, and we still climb high to cross them. Then I dip down low, and we wing across the beaches, past Silver Salmon Creek, where the abandoned set-net sites have been replaced with bear-viewing lodges. The bears still walk the beaches or drag salmon from the streams. I continue south, ascending again to cross the ridges and the saddle, where Dad and I weathered the tumultuous windstorm. Finally, I cross the last stretch of water to Augustine, where we spend the day or maybe even a night. And I tell her how my dad and I walked these sandy shores.

When I have the airplane on floats, we revisit my old hunting grounds. I land on high mountain lakes and fish for Arctic Grayling. We walk the mountains where I once walked with my dad. From high ridges, we look down on the glaciers and hear the sound of rushing water echoing in the canyons. I do all this to instill in the next generation a sense of awe and wonder at the remarkable country we live in, here in Alaska.

Along the taxiway is Memorial Hill, a gentle hill created when a CAT pushed stumps off the runway when it was first cleared. The stumps decayed into rich topsoil. Once upon a time, Mom and Dad grew straw-berries and raspberries on this hill. The strawberries escaped the plot, and their feral offspring ran free across both taxiways, the red berries, like happy surprises, peeping out from unexpected places. Even still, the raspberries offer a cup or two of harvest each season.

I inherited a love for growing things from Mom. The beauty of flowers, both wild and domestic, gives me ongoing pleasure, as does watching a vegetable garden grow and harvesting the results. Not only did she nurture strawberries and nasturtiums, but she also nurtured me. Early in life, I took her patience and unconditional love for me for granted; only later did I appreciate how deep and persistent it ran.

A tended mound at the far end of Memorial Hill, harbors two grave markers: one with Mom and Dad's names on it, the other with the name of our oldest daughter, Lindsay.

I learned so many things from my dad. I learned that if I followed him too closely through a patch of alders, I would get smacked in the face with a branch. I learned that I hated holding up log rails while he secured them to posts with bailing wire. I learned that wet floats were very slick. I learned that even though I was cold, wet, and hungry, it was not the end of the world. I also learned that standing on a mountain top was incredibly exhilarating, and while it took a lot of effort, it was worth every moment of the climb. I learned that stalking game could be as rewarding as killing game. I learned that at times there were things I did not want to do, there were things I did not choose to do, but that they were the right things to do, so I did them, just as he had. I learned that no matter how well I planned, sometimes life blew me off course, but even then, I could gain wisdom from it.

Sometimes in the fall, when I walk down the taxiway to cull a dead spruce or pick some cranberries, I am swept back in time and surrounded by clouds of memories. They swirl about like snowflakes in a blizzard, and for a moment, I am once again a kid, standing there, head back, laughing with my mouth wide open as I try to catch and savor each one. I can see my dad trudging down the same taxiway, axe over his shoulder, ready for another day of homesteading—and I miss him deeply. When I snap back to the present, I remember that even as my dad took my hand on the steep mountain slope so many decades ago, my Heavenly Father now holds my hand as I continue to travel the ups and downs of this life. And I am content.

EPILOGUE

ALTHOUGH NAOMI'S PRIMARY RESIDENCE is in Colorado, she frequently visits the Gaede-80 homestead, where she stays in the family cabin. She is the family historian and relentlessly seeks to categorize, sort, organize, document, research, and display her family's heritage. In her writing, she deliberately gives voice to teachers, missionaries, healthcare workers, Native people, and friends, many of whom have not had the ability or resources to stake written claims to their contributions.

Ruth married Roger Rupp, an Airframe and Powerplant (A&P) Aircraft mechanic. Elmer Gaede often relied on his son-in-law to repair his airplanes; later, Mark did the same. Home for Ruth is the Gaede-80 homestead. She is a seasoned homesteader and finds deep satisfaction outdoors, where she splits firewood, cleans up and burns brush, picks berries, puts in a garden, and does what it takes to establish a home in the wilderness. She never tires of seeing a moose stroll or frolic outside her window, or on the Gaede-80 grass airstrip.

In January 1980, Mishal discovered her birth mother, Dora Tooyak, in Denver, Colorado. Since then, Mishal has gracefully and gratefully integrated her biological and adopted siblings. She is adept with beadwork, various mediums of design and artwork, and sewing with furs and moose skin. Mishal lives in Fairbanks, Alaska, and is a retired Tribal Court Facilitator for Tanana Chiefs Conference, in Tribal Government Services. Being an advocate for Native people has been abundantly fulfilling for her.

Eventually, Mark and Mishal laid down their willow whips and extended the olive branch to each other. Neither ever had a pet rabbit again.

The Gaede children cherish their family's Alaska heritage.

APPRECIATION

MARK:

I would like to give credit to the friends who graced me with their time for conversations, answered questions, and confirmed that what I remembered was their shared experience as well.

+ Mom and Dad, what a resource to have your saved letters that recorded our life in Alaska. In those, I found sentences, pages, and sketches to verify my recollections, add details and descriptions, and jog my memories.
+ Jerome Near, thanks for filling in the details of my first goat hunt. I was such a little boy and had not retained some of the specifics.
+ Sandy, Mark, and David Bell, sitting around your table decades later and laughing as we recalled my summer at Silver Salmon Creek added another layer of friendship and appreciation for your family. Mark and David, your highlights coincided with mine—paper airplanes, primitive fishing spears, and matchsticks with gun shell casings. Sandy, you supplied the missing details. Boy, was I surprised to learn you were not at Silver Salmon Creek

when my dad crashed the Maule, but at the clinic when my father was brought in! I trust the chapter about your family will warm your hearts.

+ Vince and Marylil Spady, thanks for piecing together details from Camp Inowak. Oh, that my mother would have been around when I was writing that chapter so she and I could have sat together eating oatmeal cookies and reminiscing about those days.

+ Jeanne Penz Rodkey, your family loved working with the kids at Inowak, and I trust the story about that camp brings honor to your family.

+ Clark Fair, you and I have climbed many of the same mountains and immersed ourselves in Alaska's grandeur. When Naomi and I scratched our heads to identify a person qualified to edit this book, she said, "You know, for years I've read Clark Fair's columns of true-life stories on the Kenai Peninsula. He knows his stuff—the geography, flora, fauna, weather, and terminology." We pondered how to engage you in this process. We brought you coffee and homemade cinnamon rolls. You hesitated; not sure you would have the time. We didn't give up. Naomi sent you "just a few" chapters—until eventually you'd read every one. You pushed us to write more carefully, use fewer commas, and check our facts. This book is better than it ever could have been without you as our "non-editor."

NAOMI:

Storytellers can get lost in their narratives and lose readers by assuming that the excited bookworms can figure out what was implied, not actually written. That's where Critical Readers are indispensable. We gave the Critical Readers the tasks of analyzing the content, drawing to our attention redundant sentences and descriptions, informing us that a specific word had been used six times—on one page—and questioning the clarity of what we thought was already clear. We are truly grateful for Melissa Fogle and Martin Walsh who sharpened their pens on these pages.

- Melissa, your enthusiasm for these stories spurred us on.
- Martin, your methodical and questioning mind was what we'd counted on. You did not disappoint.
- I cannot thank my daughter, Nicole Penner Clark, enough. She has stood by me through decades of writing and has never groaned when I've asked her to read one page or one hundred pages "just one more time." She is an avid reader and has high standards for a better-than-good book.

RESOURCES AND FURTHER READING

BOOKS

Kenai Historical Society, compiled by. *Once Upon the Kenai*: Stories from the People. (third printing) 1985.

> Who ventures into an unsettled wilderness with rugged conditions, primitive roads, few conveniences, and, by their own muscle, resourcefulness, and a handful of kind neighbors, gains satisfaction creating a home and lifestyle? Read these captivating stories about homesteaders, doctors, missionaries, teachers, trappers, laborers, and other independent souls who settled on the (west-central) Kenai Peninsula before 1963. Dr. Elmer Gaede, one of the early physicians, got in on the last Homestead Act in the area.

Gaede-Penner, Naomi. *Alaska Bush Pilot Doctor*. Denver, CO: Prescription for Adventure, 2023.

Gaede-Penner, Naomi. *From Kansas Wheat Fields to Alaska Tundra: a Mennonite Family Finds Home.* Mustang, OK: Tate Publishing, 2014.

Gaede-Penner, Naomi. *The Bush Doctor's Wife.* Denver, CO: Prescription for Adventure, 2021.

Husby, Joan Rawlins. *Living Gold: The Story of Dave and Vera Penz of Kako, Alaska:* RainSong Press, 2018.

What brought Dave Penz to Alaska? How did his passion to serve the Native people develop? Read about Dave Penz, his family, Camp Inowak, and other Christian ministries Dave poured his heart and energy into. No matter the adversity, this indomitable man never slowed down.

Winheld, Mark. *Open the Sky: The Story of Missionary Pilot Dwayne King.* Xulon Press: 2010.

How did Dwayne King and his family show up on the Gaede's homestead as a fledgling pilot working for Missionary Aviation Repair Center in Soldotna? Read how this entry point thrust him into Christian ministries across Alaska, from starting churches to flying kids from bush villages to Bible camps. Be spellbound by these energetic, fast-paced stories.

WEBSITES

www.prescriptionforadventure.com

Check out this website for pictures of early Gaede-80 home-steading, the Gaede cabin back then and now, airplanes on the Gaede-80, and more.

www.kingdomaircorps.org

See what Dwayne is doing today.

https://www.kakoretreatcenter.org/about/

Read about Dave Penz's other camp in Alaska, where his son now carries on his legacy.

YOUTUBE
Mark Gaede's YouTube Channel:
https://youtu.be/B5l9zGLVKug?feature=shared
Or search YouTube: Mark Gaede

Babe Alsworth:
https://www.youtube.com/watch?v=oyf3DhVHhEg

MORE PRESCRIPTIONS
FOR ADVENTURE

Alaska Bush Pilot Doctor

Dr. Elmer Gaede expected to follow in the footsteps of his Mennonite farming family. He never imagined that during the 1950s and 60s, he'd fly with other legendary bush pilots, such as Babe Alsworth, Andy Anderson, Fred and John Chambers, Don Sheldon, Don Stickman, and Sig and Noel Wien; or that he'd be counted among the early Alaska physicians in Interior Alaska.

Fasten your seatbelt for his bush-flying crack-ups, fly-in house calls, and wild hunting adventures. Read how he coaxed his wife, Ruby, to shoot her first moose. Pack your sense of humor for a monkey in his clinic waiting room and delivering a baby during the 1964 Good Friday Earthquake. Recognize the hunting and flying influences on Mark's life.

The Bush Doctor's Wife

Ruby Gaede anticipated being a Kansas farmer's wife, snuggled safely into a Mennonite community with her relatives, milking cows and gathering eggs. What happens when her husband climbs off his tractor, goes to medical school, and becomes a bush pilot doctor in the middle of Alaska? She cranks homemade ice cream on the frozen Yukon River, sings Christmas carols at 40 below, and…she keeps track of Mark.

In a panic, she tracks this toddler to the mile-wide Yukon River, where he is checking on his daddy's airplane; rescues socks he flushes down the toilet; and puts out fires he starts in the house hallway. Why can't he just ride his trike in the snow and play with his daddy's moose antlers in the backyard? In all this, Ruby considers herself to be an ordinary woman.

From Kansas Wheat Fields to Alaska Tundra:
a Mennonite Family Finds Home

What is the prescription for finding a home in Alaska? Take one young Mennonite girl (Naomi) and transplant her from the flatland prairies of Kansas. Give her village potlatches, school in a Quonset hut, the fragrance of wood smoke, Native friends, a doctor-daddy who generates hunting tales and medical adventures with a small plane, and a mother with the grit to be a homesteader. Weave into her journey the perspectives of her family members, and have them face the lack of conveniences, isolation from extended family, freezing temperatures, and unknown hardships. Mix these elements with ingenuity, optimism, and a sense of adventure!

'A' is for Alaska: Teacher to the Territory

In 1954, Anna Bortel, a single woman with a teaching certificate, felt called to Valdez, Alaska, where snowfall is measured in feet, not inches. Snow sifted onto her bed, and she made a snowman atop her house. Then, she organized the first Valdez Easter Egg Hunt—in knee-deep snow. Yet, she was undaunted, and in 1957, she headed farther north, to Tanana, where she taught school and lived in drafty Quonset huts—without plumbing and with oil lines that froze at 50 below zero—and where she met Elmer and Ruby Gaede. She thought "Markie" was the cutest little kid.

'A' is for Anaktuvuk: Teacher to the Nunamiut Eskimos
A field trip to Anaktuvuk Pass with Dr. Elmer Gaede tugged at Anna Bortel's heart. The elders of the village valued education yet the conditions in their village—strong winds, no conveniences, and no transportation by dogsled or weather-permitting bush planes—were too harsh for anyone to consider teaching. They begged Anna to return as a permanent schoolteacher.

As documented in the Alaska State Legislature, Anna Bortel was the only person qualified—and willing—to accept the challenge. In this most remote village, she taught children and adults to read and write, translated Bible verses into their language, and started a craft-selling economy that enabled the people to buy food.

This book gives the Indigenous people a voice, records their history, and portrays their love for this indomitable, compassionate woman.

Whether chosen or unchosen, all these people
had a prescription for adventure.

What is your prescription for adventure?

INDEX